So You Want To Be Selling Sunsets...

BARRY PULVER

Do you know why you want to get into real estate?

YES ☐

NO ☐

OTHER ☐

Do you know your definition of success in real estate?

YES ☐

NO ☐

OTHER ☐

Table of contents

Introduction — 4

Chapter 1: The Lure of the Property Horizon — 7
- Why Real Estate? — 7
- The Financial Incentives — 11
- The Entrepreneurial Spirit — 15

Chapter 2: Laying the Groundwork — 19
- Understanding the Market — 19
- Building a Robust Network — 24
- Developing the Right Skills — 28

Chapter 3: Navigating Legalities and Ethics — 38
- Real Estate Law 101 — 38
- Ethical Selling: A Must — 41
- Every State Is Different — 44

Chapter 4: The Journey to Licensure — 45
- The Licensing Exam: A Blueprint — 45
- Choosing Your Brokerage — 49
- Continuing Education and Growth — 53

Chapter 5: Choosing the Right Fit — 58
- Understanding Your Goals and Values — 58
- Researching Potential Brokerages — 65
- Interviewing Brokerages — 69
- Considering Mentorship and Support — 77
- Making the Final Decision — 80

Chapter 6: Making the Sale – The Art and Science — 97
- Time Out — 97
- Mastering the Showing — 98
- Negotiation Tactics for Winners — 102
- Closing the Deal — 109

Chapter 7: Our Gift to You — 113
- We Are Here for You — 113

Introduction

It's Friday night, you turn on Netflix and you decide to watch a show where everyone is good looking, having fun, yet full of drama... and occasionally showing and selling homes where the commission is well above $100,00 EACH sale. Sound familiar?

Well they make it look easy, so if they can do it on Selling Sunset, then why should you not be looking to be selling your own sunsets...

We welcome you to a tale, both with a glimpse of illusive freedom from the corporate world, the other with the first hurdle you have to jump high through before that snapshot can even be explored. Both with both in mind, we welcome you to this book which is a combination of many factors, all designed to challenge your thought process and desire of whether the allure of real estate is one you want to genuinely give it all you have.

My journey as chief and editor of this read, Barry Pulver has been a unique one which as opposed to what you will forever hear in real estate "do not re-invent the wheel", I took the other road and upon finding the right alignment have done things even imaginable to me as I write these words. So along with much research, the wonderful power and imagination of technology and artificial intelligence, we combine to share a journey of an average real estate agent who went from being a capping agent to a global team leader with over $1 billion in annual homes sales, in just a few years. This message serves to say that even if the odds are not on your side, the unimaginable is possible and that we where we begin this journey together...

The problem is simple: many enter the fray armed with nothing but desires, lacking the armor of knowledge and strategy.

Picture this: those million dollar listings are the ambitions of many, a place where the unprepared see their aspirations crumble like sandcastles against the relentless tide of reality. Why do you want to scale these opulent heights? Can you weather the storm of a market that ebbs and flows with the caprice of a tempest? In the pages that follow, I will guide you through the labyrinth. Prepare to step onto a path less traveled, where the secrets of a billion-dollar legacy await. But be warned, not all is as it seems in the world of high stakes and open houses. Will you have what it takes to unlock the grandeur of selling sunsets? The answer lies just beyond the horizon, where the sky meets the sea in a blaze of glory. And there... we will begin.

In the glow of the setting sun, where dreams are as tangible as the sprawling properties that line the shore, the world of real estate beckons like the ultimate frontier—a land of promise and prosperity. Yet, as the number one global real estate agent, I've witnessed firsthand the chasm that yawns between aspiration and reality.

The real estate industry in America is a mosaic of breathtaking possibilities and daunting challenges. It's an arena where only the most tenacious and knowledgeable thrive. You see, the problem isn't a lack of opportunity; it's an abundance of naivety. Too many enter the fray, bewitched by the allure of grandeur and wealth, only to falter at the first hurdle, unprepared for the rigors this world demands.

Imagine the crushing weight of expectation giving way beneath the gravity of the market's complexity. Consider the heartbreak of countless individuals like you who have embarked on this journey, only to find themselves lost in a labyrinth of legalities, negotiations, and an ever-shifting property landscape. The fallout is not just personal; the ripples extend to every dream home left unsold, every family's future put on hold.

Let me tell you about Samantha. A bright-eyed, ambitious soul, Samantha came to me after her spirit was nearly broken by the industry. She had passion, a vision of herself triumphantly staging homes against the canvas of golden sunsets. Yet, without the right preparation and understanding, her vision was just that—a mirage. Samantha's story is not unique, but it's one I bring to our journey as a beacon, a warning, and a catalyst for change.

This is about more than just selling properties; it's about shaping lives. Your success or failure in real estate reverberates through the lives of those you touch—clients, families, communities. The stakes? They couldn't be higher. We're talking about the bedrock of the American dream: homeownership. To falter is to fail those who entrust you with their aspirations. To succeed is to be an architect of dreams.

In these pages, I will unveil the roadmap to a career painted in success. From the whys to the hows, we will navigate every twist and turn together. I will share with you the strategies that helped me sell over a billion dollars of homes a year, the insights that stretch across continents and cultures. You will learn not just how to get your real estate license, but how to wield it with finesse and integrity.

Why do you want to scale these opulent heights?

Can you weather the storm of a market that ebbs and flows with the caprice of a tempest?

It's time to look beyond the allure, beyond the sunsets. I challenge you to focus on the 'why'—the driving force behind your ambition. Is it the thrill of the chase, the joy of making dreams a reality, or the siren call of wealth? Pinpoint your purpose, for it will be your compass in the tumultuous seas of real estate.

From the foundations of your aspirations to the pinnacle of your first sale, my guidance will be your beacon. Together, we will dissect the industry's intricacies, build your arsenal of knowledge, and hone your skills to a razor's edge.

So, take a deep breath. The path ahead is lined with the silhouettes of dreams and the shadows of giants. But remember, in the world of real estate, the brightest light comes from the sun setting on a deal well done. Welcome to your journey of selling sunsets. Welcome to the blueprint of a billion-dollar legacy. Welcome to the beginning.

The answer lies just beyond the horizon, where the sky meets the sea in a blaze of glory.

And there... we will begin.

Chapter 1: The Lure of the Property Horizon

Why Real Estate?

Real estate, in its essence, is the very ground upon which we build our lives—both literally and metaphorically. It's a term that gets bandied about with such frequency that its profound significance can sometimes be overlooked. So let's take a moment to peel back the layers of this familiar concept.

Let's be honest, whether in the UK or in the US, everyone always wants to talk about two things, the weather and houses. When people know you are a real estate agent (the very goal of being an agent) the one question you will forever hear more than any other is "so, how's the market?"

At its core, real estate refers to property consisting of land and the buildings on it, along with its natural resources such as crops, minerals, or water. But to leave it at that would be an injustice to its complexity and influence. Real estate is also the realm of rights, interests, and the air above the land. It extends to include the intricate transactions, the legalities of ownership, and the emotional weight a piece of property can hold as a home, a heritage, or a haven for future dreams.

To fully appreciate the depth of real estate, one might look at its etymological roots—'real' stemming from the Latin word 'res', meaning 'things', and 'estate' referring to the state or condition of the things. This is a sphere where the tangible and intangible converge, where the solidity of the ground beneath our feet meets the fluidity of market forces and human aspirations.

Situated within the broader framework of the economy, real estate is both a driver and a reflector of financial health. It's an industry that responds to and influences everything from interest rates to job growth, from consumer confidence to the machinations of global markets.

The real-world applications of real estate are as varied as the landscapes it encompasses. From the urban developer revitalizing a downtown core to the rural agent helping a family find their first home; from the luxury market mavens in high-powered cities to the property managers ensuring the seamless operation of rental spaces—real estate is a mosaic of professions, people, and purposes.

A common misconception is that a career in real estate is simply about buying and selling property. However, the truth is that it encompasses a myriad of roles—appraisers, inspectors, counselors, educators, negotiators, MOST IMPORTANT - marketers, and more. Each one requires a unique skill set, a keen understanding of human behavior, and, above all, an unwavering commitment to ethics and excellence.

Why, then, do individuals choose a path in real estate? Is it the vision of Netflix shows and big pay cheques, the promise of prosperity, or the deeper yearning to be part of someone's story of finding a place to call home? It's perhaps all of these and more.

Consider the thrill that comes from orchestrating a deal where all parties leave the table beyond satisfied, the pride in knowing you've played a part in a milestone of someone's life, or the strategic excitement in navigating the ever-shifting sands of the housing market.

But let's not wander through this garden of potential without acknowledging the thorns. Challenges are as inherent to real estate as they are to any worthwhile pursuit. Market fluctuations, economic downturns, and regulatory changes are but a few of the hurdles that must be cleared. Yet, for those with the right blend of tenacity, knowledge, and passion, these hurdles aren't barriers—they're stepping stones.

[Did you know the NAR (National Association of Realtors) statistic that over 80% of real estate agents leave the industry within the first 2 years? No? Well, this is a particular mission of mine to stop this trend, create more transparency from the start (hence this book) and set people up for success!]

So, what drives you? Is it the thought of the palpable energy of an open house, the meticulous craft of staging, the adrenaline of closing a hard-fought negotiation, or perhaps the simple, profound joy of handing over the keys to a pair of wide-eyed new homeowners?

Let us be clear: embarking on a career in real estate is not a decision to be made lightly. It demands a dedication to learning, an openness to growth, and a resilience that can weather the storms of uncertainty. But for those who choose this path, the rewards can be as boundless as the horizon.

In the coming chapters, we'll dissect the anatomy of a successful real estate career. We'll explore the nuances of market analysis, the artistry of client relations, and the science of property law. Each facet will be examined with the precision of a master jeweler, ensuring that by the time you turn the final page, you'll not only understand the 'why' but possess the arguably more important 'how'.

The real estate landscape is vast and varied, a reflection of humanity's diversity and dreams. As you stand at its threshold, ask yourself: Do you yearn for the rush of victory, the satisfaction of service, or the lure of legacy? Your answer to 'Why Real Estate?' is the key that unlocks the door to your future.

And with that key in hand, we step forward into the heart of our journey. Together, we will traverse the vast plains of potential, scale the heights of ambition, and delve deep into the bedrock of knowledge. The path ahead is not for the faint-hearted. But for those with the courage to walk it and be consistent, the rewards are immeasurable.

The sun dips below the horizon, the day's last light illuminating the path before you—a path lined with dreams yet to be realized and destinies yet to be fulfilled. Walk it with purpose, walk it with passion.

And there... we will continue.

The Financial Incentives

As we see from the real estate TV shows we stream (yes I said we, guilty!) you walk into the office, the owner hands you a $7 million listing, you sell it in 30 days, you ring the bell and you take home 50% of the commission... simple and easy right?

In the realistic realm of real estate, your potential earnings are as expansive as the properties you deal with. The level of success you will have will depend on your commitment, willingness to learn, focus on your own niche and personal branding and who you align yourself with as a company, but more importantly a mentor.

Real estate offers lucrative financial benefits that stem from commission structures, market growth potential, not forgetting a plethora of investment opportunities and residual income opportunities, but these are not the main focus of this book.

Let's delve into the first supporting evidence for this claim—the commission structure. In real estate, commissions are the lifeblood of the broker's earnings, a percentage-based reward for the successful matchmaking of buyer and seller. Here, the numbers speak for themselves. Real estate transactions over the last 5 years have on average shown real estate commission ranges from 5 to 6 percent of the property's sale price, which, when dealing with the median U.S. home value, translates into a substantial sum. Imagine the closing of a deal on a $300,000 home; a 6 percent commission would yield an $18,000 payout. And that's just one transaction. Multiply this by the number of deals a dedicated agent can close in a year, and the earnings can be staggering.

The typical misconnception with these numbers though if that more often than not you will be representing one side of the deal, so that $18,000 at a 3% fee is $9,000 and the split of your real estate company / brokerage will vary from 50-80% typically, equaling as low as $4,500.

[Bare in mind at the very moment of writing this book, the NAR have lost a court case of in essence there being set numbers and figures of buyer agency commission. Just to add that personally, I feel the whole dynamic of a real estate buyer agent will be drastically different in the year 2030 and beyond, more like what our partners do in Australia. We can definitely help set you up for success with this at a later time, but for now this note is just to add that there is no 'normal' or 'typical' commission in real estate].

But the allure doesn't end with commissions. The real estate market is dynamic, often riding the waves of economic growth, with property values appreciating over time. For instance, historical data from the Federal Housing Finance Agency indicates that average home prices have increased by approximately 3.5 percent per year since the 1970s. This was vastly expedited too during the "Covid years". This appreciation represents not just a win for homeowners but a boon for savvy real estate professionals who invest in the market. The potential for capital gains is a potent draw, inviting those with an eye for trends and a knack for timing to partake in the market's growth.

Of course, one cannot extol the virtues of real estate's financial incentives without acknowledging the counter-evidence. Critics point out the volatility of the housing market, citing events like the 2008 financial crisis, which saw property values plummet and left many in the industry reeling. They argue that reliance on commissions can result in an unstable income, subject to the whims of the market and economic cycles.

However, this counterargument only serves to emphasize the importance of market literacy and diversification within the industry. The seasoned real estate professional understands the cyclical nature of the market and prepares for lean times during periods of abundance. Moreover, the very volatility that critics highlight is also a source of opportunity for those who can adeptly navigate the ebbs and flows of the market, buying low and selling high.

In addition to direct sales commissions and capital gains from property appreciation, real estate also offers investment opportunities through rental income. This additional supporting evidence points to the steady stream of passive income that can be generated by owning and renting out properties. According to the U.S. Census Bureau, the national average rental vacancy rate in the fourth quarter of 2020 was 6.5 percent, indicating a strong demand for rental properties. By purchasing and managing rental units, real estate professionals can establish a consistent revenue source that complements transaction-based earnings.

Concluding with a reinforced assertion, it's evident that the financial incentives of real estate are compelling. They present a tapestry of potential earnings through commissions, appreciation, and rental income, woven together by the skilled hands of those who understand and respect the market's intricacies.

As you ponder the path of 'selling sunsets', does the prospect of financial freedom stir your soul? Can you envision a life where your income mirrors the boundless skies above the properties you represent? Real estate offers a canvas upon which your financial dreams can be painted, limited only by your ambition and expertise.

So, as we turn our gaze toward the horizon where opportunity awaits, let us step confidently forward, knowing that the financial incentives of real estate are not just a mirage but a tangible reality attainable by those willing to master the art of the deal AND separate themselves from the rest through personal branding.

And now, as the day advances, we must prepare to explore the strategic foundations upon which successful real estate careers are built. The financial incentives are clear; the question remains—how will you seize them? The answer lies in the following pages, a guide to harnessing the tools and tactics necessary to thrive in this lucrative field. Stay the course, for the journey is as rewarding as the destination.

The Entrepreneurial Spirit

In the tapestry of modern careers, few endeavors capture the essence of the entrepreneurial spirit quite like the real estate industry. It stands as a testament to the power of independence, the beauty of creativity, and the exhilarating rush that comes from carving one's own path. Yet, within this realm of opportunity, there lies a significant issue that must be addressed to ensure success in this competitive field.

Let's go one step further and be honest with ourselves… what over industry can you effectively control your own destiny and be a business owner for under a $2,000 upfront investment (fees, licenses, schooling etc) and months' worth of (now especially) on-line schooling?

The real estate market, though ripe with potential, is also fraught with challenges that can hinder the unprepared entrepreneur. These are what I really want to emphasize for you reading the book, because setting the right expectation is key to a successful career as a real estate agent. The primary challenge lies in the unpredictability of the market, the complexity of property transactions, the fact that everyone knows at least 25 other real estate agents and the sheer amount of knowledge required to thrive. Without a solid foundation and the right mentorship by your side, many aspiring real estate professionals find themselves overwhelmed, unable to navigate the intricacies of the industry.

If left unaddressed, these challenges could lead to more than just personal setbacks. They can result in financial losses, tarnished reputations, and missed opportunities. The consequences are not limited to the individual but can ripple outward, affecting clients, colleagues, and the market as a whole. Ultimately the previous NAR statistic of new agents leaving the industry makes a lot more sense now!

The solution to these challenges is multifold, beginning with a commitment to education and continuous learning. Prospective real estate entrepreneurs must immerse themselves in the market's nuances, understanding the economic factors that drive property values, the legalities of transactions, and the strategies for beyond effective marketing and negotiation.

Implementing this educational approach requires a structured plan. First, one must seek out reputable sources of information, such as certified courses, experienced mentors, and industry literature. Next, it's crucial to apply the acquired knowledge through practical experience, starting sometimes with smaller deals others are unwilling to take and gradually taking on more complex transactions as one's confidence and competence grow.

Evidence of the efficacy of this approach can be seen in the stories of successful real estate moguls who attribute their accomplishments to lifelong learning and hands-on experience. They often speak of early failures as invaluable lessons that propelled them to greater heights.

My own experience in this field is exactly my reason for wanting you to read the book. Even with a few years of real estate under my belt, I took the biggest gamble and leap of my career in the summer of 2018 when I moved to a newer less known brokerage. Fortunately for me, with the right alignment, mentorship and support, I ended up taking that company (now the largest independent real estate company in the world) international and am the #1 team leader in the world.

While education and experience stand as the pillars of this proposed solution, alternative strategies also merit consideration. For instance, leveraging technology can streamline processes and provide analytical tools that aid decision-making. Networking with professionals from various sectors can offer insights and opportunities that might otherwise remain out of reach.

Dive deep into the heart of the industry, and picture the bustling city centers, the serene suburban landscapes, and the untapped potential of each property. Envision the entrepreneur, standing before a canvas of endless possibilities, paintbrush in hand, ready to create a masterpiece of success. It's a scene rife with promise, where the only limits are those of one's ambition and willingness to learn.

Do you feel the pull, the desire to join the ranks of those who shape skylines and forge communities? Can you commit to the journey of discovery that lies at the core of this entrepreneurial venture?

Real estate is not just a business; it's a craft. It requires the finesse of an artist, the mind of a strategist, and the heart of an explorer. Quotes from industry veterans often echo this sentiment, declaring that each deal is a story, each property a character, and each closing a satisfying conclusion to a well-written chapter.

So, let us embark on this journey, not as passive bystanders but as active participants in the narrative of real estate. Let each step forward be a stroke of the brush, each learned lesson a hue added to our palette. With education as our guide and experience as our teacher, the entrepreneurial spirit will lead us to success, selling not just properties, but also the dreams of sunsets that captivate and inspire.

As the sun sets, casting a final warm glow on the city, the day's end signals not a conclusion, but an anticipation of the dawn to come. For the true entrepreneur, the journey never ends; it evolves, presenting new challenges and new opportunities with each rising sun.

Chapter 2: Laying the Groundwork

Understanding the Market

Embarking on the journey to be selling those sunsets is akin to navigating a labyrinth; it demands an acute understanding of the ever-shifting patterns that paint the horizon of the real estate market. Your objective? To become proficient in reading these patterns, assessing the true worth of properties, and grasping the economic levers that sculpt the industry's contours.

Before you set out, ensure you're equipped with the essentials: a blend of analytical tools, access to current and historical market data, a network of knowledgeable industry contacts, a mentor and a mindset ready to absorb and adapt. These prerequisites are the compass and map that will guide you through the terrain ahead.

Imagine a tapestry on which the broad strokes of market trends, property values, and economic forces are interwoven. We'll delve into the intricacies of each thread, learning to distinguish the subtle nuances that make the difference between a seasoned seller and an uninitiated one.

Let's begin by unfolding the market trends. Picture a wave in the ocean, its rise and fall influenced by a multitude of factors, from interest rates to employment figures. Here, we observe the long-term patterns, noticing how the tide of buyer sentiment ebbs and flows, and how seasonality can affect demand.

Transition to the granular details of assessing property values. Every home has a story told through its architecture, its wear, and the laughter once shared within its walls. You'll learn to listen to these stories and translate them into numbers, understanding the fine balance between the sentimental and the fiscal.

Now, envisage the economic forces as winds that propel the market's sails. Interest rates, inflation, a global pandemic, worldwide wars and government policies are but a few gusts that can alter the course. Recognize these winds, and you'll harness them, using the knowledge to steer your decisions.

A top agent will actually be making more money during the down times as their focus on their own local market in addition to personal branding will stand out about the 99% of agents who are working in their business and not on it.

Throughout your journey, heed these tips: stay vigilant of market indicators, network relentlessly, and always—always—have your clients' best interests at heart. A word of warning: avoid the trap of emotional pricing; let data and facts guide your valuations.

To verify your mastery, apply your newfound insights. Analyze a property, predict its trajectory in the current market, and outline a strategy. If the results align with your predictions, you're charting the course correctly.

Should you encounter rough seas—a misjudged market trend or an overestimated property value—retrace your steps. Review the data, consult your network, and adjust your sail.

How do you know the difference between these two?

Experience for one is always going to be the best judge and sail, however it once again re-emphasizes the true importance of a business partner and mentorship guiding and assisting you along the seven seas with each change of the course of direction.

Now, let us embark on this chapter of your story, one filled with the promise of golden horizons and the satisfaction of a journey well-navigated.

Have you ever stood before the vast expanse of the real estate market, wondering where to cast your gaze first? How can one discern a burgeoning neighborhood from a declining one, or the potential of a property that others have overlooked?

For me in recent memory watching so many property taxes almost double within two years of covid in the small market of Davidson, North Carolina was a very eye opening experience. Added to that interest rates rising from sub 3% to over 7% in the same time frame, with inventory still low, NOT a typical cycle for real estate in any historical time.

The tools at hand—a market analysis software, a trusty calculator, and a ledger of contacts—are the first steps in carving a path to success. Yet, as always, it's not just what you have, but how you use them. A software can churn out numbers, but can you read the story they tell?

Seize a broad view of the market. What are the trending areas? Where is the development booming? This overview is your first foray into understanding where the sun might set most profitably for your clients.

Now, dissect these trends. Begin with the macroeconomic indicators; they are the pulse you need to feel. Is the general economy thriving, or is it in a slump? How are the interest rates behaving? These factors are like the tide, influencing all ships in the sea of the market.

Zoom in further. The neighborhood's quality of schools, the walkability, the local amenities—these are the tangible aspects that breathe value into a property. But don't overlook the intangible—the potential for community, the sense of belonging, the quietude or vibrancy of a street. These too wield power in the market's grand scale.

Consider this: a home is not merely a construction of bricks and beams—it's a canvas where lives are painted. How you represent this to buyers can make all the difference. [This for me is my favorite part of real estate!]

And as you navigate this intricate process, remember to ask yourself poignant questions. Are you considering all variables? Have you consulted the historical data? Are you letting numbers speak, or are biases whispering too loudly?

Use adjectives with intention, and adverbs sparingly. A house isn't just large; it's sprawling, with room to grow dreams. And it isn't merely well-located; it sits at the heart of everything, a stone's throw from life's conveniences.

A one-line paragraph for emphasis: The market waits for no one.

Craft your sentences with rhythm, a dance of words that carries your reader through the complexity with ease. And when a quote fits snugly, use it to lend authority to your insights.

Remember to show, not tell. Don't just state that a market is growing; illustrate it with the buzz of new construction, the opening of chic cafes, the influx of young families scouting for their forever homes.

In the end, real estate is not just about the transaction. It's about the understanding that you are not merely selling properties, but futures, dreams, and the stage for life's many sunrises and sunsets.

You are selling yourself.

Building a Robust Network

In the dynamic dance of real estate, each step is measured by the strength of your connections. It's a world where the currency of success is not just properties traded but the robustness of your network. Take a moment and ask yourself, have you truly invested in this currency?

You know the cliche "Your net work is your net worth", feel free to roll your eyes, but after you have, do understand that there is more truth in that phrase than you know. Going back to the title and inspiration of this book and our 'favorite' Netflix streaming real estate show, how is it, some brand new agent can walk into an uber competition market like Beverly Hills and they already (straight from the real estate license office) have a $20 million buyer they are working with? Exactly! Who you know, more importantly who knows YOU is honestly more important than how good of a real estate agent you are.

Controversial? Yes, True? You'll see...

Imagine a marketplace, a bustling agora of the ancient world. Here, traders and townsfolk converse, deals are struck, and the air is thick with the potential of prosperity. Your journey in real estate is not so different. The marketplace is your community, and your success hinges on the vibrancy of your interactions within it.

Yet, a significant challenge emerges: the real estate terrain is notoriously competitive and can be isolating. Agents often find themselves as lone wolves, scouring the market for leads, clawing for listings, and guarding their territory. But in this solitary pursuit, they neglect the power of collective wisdom and the opportunities that come with a shared horizon.

Consider the fate of the lone wolf when the winter of market downturns arrives. Without a pack, without a network, the chill of isolation creeps in. Opportunities become scarce, and one's ability to weather the storm is compromised. The consequences? Stagnation, loss of revenue, and the dimming of the once-promising glow of a real estate career.

The antidote lies in the creation of a network, a constellation of clients, mentors, colleagues, and industry professionals. A network that not only refers business but also provides insight, support, and camaraderie. This network becomes your tribe, your go-to resource, your foundation.

[This above for me personally was the key to my success and the joy continued to be found every single day (yes challenges included) and our love of real estate. Our hope in this book ultimately is that you decide you truly do want to embark upon real estate as a career and one step further that you take us up on our exclusive offer of mentorship and conversation at the end of this book. One very powerful statement we look at and are reminder of daily (with thanks to JFK) is that "a rising tide lifts all boats" let this be YOU.]

But how does one cultivate such a network? The first step is to engage genuinely with clients. See them not as transactions but as relationships to nurture. Each satisfied client becomes a beacon, illuminating your reputation in the market, leading to repeat and referred business.

Next, seek mentors (hello again, my name is Barry Pulver!) . These are the seasoned navigators of real estate, whose compasses have found true north. They can offer guidance, help you avoid pitfalls, and when the time comes, advocate for your character and skills.

Do not overlook your peers. They may be competitors, but they are also potential collaborators. Co-listing, sharing market insights, business partners and supporting each other's successes can lead to a thriving community of practice. This is not common, but for the top agents and those of us considered in this bracket, this could not be more true.

Be present in industry events. Each handshake, each exchange of business cards is a seed planted, which with care, can grow into a flourishing partnership.

Evidence of this approach's efficacy is commonly found in the stories of top-performing agents. Their careers are tapestries woven with the threads of countless interactions, each connection contributing to a resilient and enduring career.

Certainly, there are other strategies. Playing devil's advocate, we would argue for a strong online presence, others for aggressive marketing tactics. While these have a foundational place in your business (a conversation for another time), they still lack the human element, the personal touch that turns a service into a lifelong relationship.

In the end, remember this truth: real estate is as much about people as it is about properties. It is a social endeavor, and your network is the soil in which your career will grow and flourish. So ask yourself, are you ready to plant the seeds that will become your forest of opportunities? Are you ready to be not just a seller of sunsets but a cultivator of connections?

Developing the Right Skills

In the realm of real estate, selling sunsets is as much an art as it is a science. To excel, one must possess a plethora of skills, each thread interwoven with expertise and finesse. But what are these skills, and why do they matter? As you delve into the pages that follow, you will uncover the essential competencies that set apart the novices from the maestros in this competitive landscape.

Before one can master the art of real estate, a clear understanding of the necessary skills is paramount. These are not just tools in your arsenal but the very pillars upon which a successful career is built.

The key skills every real estate professional should cultivate include:

1. Negotiation Mastery
2. Marketing Ingenuity
3. Industry Knowledge
4. Technological Proficiency
5. Exceptional Communication
6. Legal and Ethical Adherence
7. Emotional Intelligence
8. Time Management and Organization
9. Networking Prowess
10. Personal Branding

Negotiation Mastery

Negotiation is the heartbeat of real estate dealings. It is where interests collide and deals are birthed. A master negotiator knows it's not about conquest but about finding the harmony of mutual satisfaction. They understand the psychology behind the process, the dance of give-and-take, and they listen intently to grasp the unspoken needs of their counterpart.

Evidence of effective negotiation is found in the stories of agents who have turned seemingly impossible scenarios into wins for all parties involved. Testimonials from clients often highlight the ability of their agent to secure deals that seemed just out of reach.

Practical application of this skill can be seen during a bidding war, where a real estate agent must balance the needs of the seller with the limits of potential buyers, finding a sweet spot that satisfies both sides.

The two most important factors in the art of negotiation are remembering you are working exclusively for your client and your fiduciary duties (these words will forever haunt you from your real estate pre-licensing class) are always with them. Not forgetting that the true psychology and art of winning a negotiation and deal is truly wanting a win-win for all parties involved.

Marketing Ingenuity

In an era where attention is fragmented (hello social media and instant gratification), marketing ingenuity stands out as a beacon. It's the art of crafting compelling narratives around properties, of making a home more than just a structure but a dream, a possibility.

Anecdotes from successful campaigns demonstrate the power of innovative marketing. A home that languished on the market, ignored, can transform into the most sought-after residence with the right story woven around it.

Apply this ingenuity in staging homes, in creating breathtaking virtual tours, and in leveraging social media to reach potential buyers on a platform they frequent.

A not so popular viewpoint that I always say to my mentees around the world is that truly what we are selling in real estate is not our clients, not the homes but ourselves. [We will get more into this in the personal branding section]

Industry Knowledge

A well of industry knowledge is indispensable. It's the foundation that informs all other skills. This encompasses understanding market trends, property laws, and the economic factors that influence real estate.

Industry publications and market analyses provide evidence of the ever-changing landscape, highlighting the importance of staying informed.

In practice, this knowledge allows you to advise clients on when to sell or buy, what investments to consider, and how to interpret market data.

Think big, market big but be hyper local and dialed in to your local town, local market and local community. As discussed before, know the macro when it comes to industry trends but ultimately what a home seller / buyer is wanting to know is what directly effects them... that is what is happening **where** they live.

Technological Proficiency

Technology is reshaping the real estate world. From virtual showings to blockchain contracts, the future is digital. Technological proficiency means not just understanding these tools but using them to create seamless experiences for clients.

Success stories abound of agents who leveraged technology to expand their reach, using virtual reality to show homes to international clients, or employing data analytics to target the right audience.

Incorporate this skill by adopting the latest software for customer relationship management (CRM) and by creating an online presence that showcases your properties and services.

[There would be no way without this that I could personally run an international network spanning from Wales to Australia and a total of 6 continents. The key word when it comes to technology and even AI is how and what can you leverage specifically for building and growing your business. Fortunately, I can help you directly in this area]

Exceptional Communication

The linchpin of all real estate transactions (even life) is communication. It is the thread that connects every stage of the buying or selling process. Whether it's articulating the benefits of a property or explaining complex legal documents, clarity, and confidence in communication are non-negotiable.

Client feedback often cites clear communication as a decisive factor in choosing an agent. The ability to simplify the jargon and keep all parties informed creates trust and leads to smoother transactions.

Practice this skill by always keeping clients updated, using various communication channels to suit their preferences, and by being an active listener.

The toughest conversations, you know, the ones you do not want to have (we have all been there) are arguably and often the ones that will get you that client, get the offer accepted and grow your business. Remember setting the expectation is a fundamental in real estate and sometimes re-setting those expectations will enhance your reputation!

Legal and Ethical Adherence

Adhering to legal and ethical standards is not merely a requirement but the bedrock of your reputation. This means being well-versed in the laws governing real estate and holding oneself to the highest ethical standards.

Instances of litigation against agents who have flouted these standards serve as cautionary tales, emphasizing the need for integrity in every action.

Demonstrate this in your practice by ensuring all documentation is accurate and legally compliant, and by treating all parties with fairness and respect.

This is in place for the national level and state level where there might and likely will be differences.

Emotional Intelligence

The ability to navigate the emotional landscape of clients is a subtle yet powerful skill. It's about empathy, understanding the stresses and joys that come with buying or selling a home.

Testimonials often highlight an agent's emotional intelligence, praising their support and guidance through the emotional rollercoaster of real estate transactions.

Enhance this ability by being attuned to your client's feelings, offering support during difficult decisions, and celebrating their successes with genuine and authentic warmth.

Time Management and Organization

In the whirlwind of showings, meetings, marketing and paperwork, time management and organization emerge as vital skills. They allow you to juggle multiple clients and deadlines without dropping the ball OR losing focus on the most important part of your business, getting more business!

Agents who excel in this area often share their systems and tools that keep them on track, from digital calendars, peer accountability to task management apps.

To apply these skills, prioritize tasks based on urgency and importance, create a structured daily routine, and maintain meticulous records of all interactions and transactions.

Know how you work best and what you need for accountability, can you keep yourself accountable? Or do you need your mentor to?

Networking Prowess

Again; "Your network is your net worth" in real estate. It's about building relationships that lead to opportunities and referrals.

The success stories of top agents frequently include mentions of how their network was instrumental in their achievements, whether it was a tip about an upcoming listing or an introduction to a potential client.

Practice networking by attending industry events, joining professional groups, and staying in touch with past clients and colleagues.

On the other end of the spectrum there are always events you will be invited to. It is very important to be very specific and strategic for which ones are your priority and not get overwhelmed by always attending events and never taking action.

Personal Branding

Lastly, personal branding sets you apart in a crowded market. It's about defining who you are as an agent and what unique value you offer, with nothing but true authenticity.

Agents with a strong personal brand are easily recognizable, their names synonymous with certain types of properties or a specific level of service.

Craft your personal brand by being consistent in your messaging, by showcasing your successes, and by aligning your public image with your personal values and professional strengths.

This is our passion and joy and maybe it is because of the success attained can be pin pointed back to where the focus and time went into creating our own personal brand.

As you embark on refining these skills, remember that they are not static. They evolve as you do, growing in depth and breadth with each transaction, each interaction. It's a journey of continuous improvement, with the horizon of your potential ever-expanding. So, are you ready to step into the grand amphitheater of real estate with these skills as your script, ready to play the lead role in the epic tale of selling sunsets?

Chapter 3: Navigating Legalities and Ethics

Real Estate Law 101

Venturing into the vibrant world of real estate transactions, one must first navigate the intricate web of property law, contracts, and regulations that serve as the framework of this bustling marketplace. To sell those sunsets effectively, you'll need more than just an eye for beauty and negotiation skills; you must also grasp the legalities that confirm ownership and facilitate fair, enforceable agreements. Fortunately this is a large part of the pre-licensing course and the hoops you have to go through to officially call yourself a real estate license.

Understanding real estate law is akin to studying the rules of a complex game—one where stakes run high and the playing field spans from dusty deeds in courthouse archives to the sleek digital signatures on contemporary contracts. At its core, this body of law encompasses the rights and duties of parties involved in the purchase, possession, use, and sale of real estate.

But what exactly does it mean to have a right to a piece of property? Let's delve deeper. Ownership rights in property law are often described as a bundle of sticks, each stick representing a different right or interest. These can include the right to possess, to use, to exclude others, to profits from the land, and even the right to destroy or alter it. Yet, these are not absolute; they are subject to zoning laws, environmental regulations, and other governmental restrictions.

Consider the scenario of a young couple excited to transform an old farmhouse into their dream home. They must navigate zoning ordinances that dictate land use, building codes that set construction standards, and sometimes historical preservation rules that preserve the character of certain properties. These layers of regulation ensure that individual decisions about property use contribute to the overall welfare and aesthetic of the community.

Now, let us examine the contract—a pivotal document in any real estate transaction. A contract in this context is an agreement between a buyer and a seller that outlines the terms of the property transfer. It must be in writing to be enforceable and typically includes details such as the purchase price, description of the property, and any contingencies that must be met before the sale can conclude.

In real estate, contingencies are not mere trivialities; they're critical ifs that can make or break a sale. Imagine a home with a hidden flaw, like a cracked foundation. A savvy buyer would include an inspection contingency, ensuring they can back out or renegotiate if significant defects are uncovered.

Across the spectrum, perspectives on regulatory elements vary. Some argue that stringent regulations stifle creativity and economic growth, while others believe they are vital to protecting both individual and public interests. A developer may decry the red tape that delays construction, while a neighbor celebrates the same regulations for preserving their community's charm.

To bolster our exploration, consider this: in the United States, over 5 million existing homes were sold in 2021 alone, according to the National Association of Realtors. This staggering number not only illustrates the scale of real estate transactions but also underscores the importance of a solid legal foundation to support this volume of commerce.

It's vital to clarify complex terms like "easement," which grants the right to use another's property for a specific purpose—say, a pathway across one property to reach another. Or "lien," a legal claim on a property due to unpaid debts, which can derail a sale if not properly addressed.

To encapsulate the essence of real estate law, consider these key takeaways: it is the sinew that connects the bones of commerce, a dynamic interplay of rights and regulations that must be understood to facilitate smooth transactions. A robust knowledge of this legal framework not only empowers agents and buyers but also fosters trust, ensuring that each golden hour ushers in a fair and fruitful exchange.

Rightly or wrongly, ever real estate agent in America is required to take annual CE (Continuing Education) courses and 50% of this is in regarding the laws, paperwork / documentation changes that are taking effect for the upcoming year. Again, states might vary, in North Carolina, there are two 4 hour courses required every year, 4 hours is the mandatory class described above and the second 4 hours can be chosen from a variety of subjects.

In closing, ask yourself: are you ready to wield the gavel of knowledge, to turn the key of understanding that unlocks the doors to selling sunsets with confidence and legal acumen? Remember, in the domain of real estate, the law is not just a set of rules; it is the very foundation upon which the industry stands.

Ethical Selling: A Must

In the delicate dance of real estate, where dreams are traded with handshakes and fortunes hinge on signatures, there lies a truth often whispered but seldom acknowledged. It is the cornerstone of longevity and the hallmark of the truly successful: ethical practices in selling properties are not just commendable; they are essential.

The bustling world of real estate is rife with opportunity and fraught with temptation. Agents, in their quest to close deals and clients eager to claim their slice of paradise, may find themselves at a crossroads where integrity is tested. Here, we examine the crux of the matter: the frequent divergence from ethical paths and its potential to erode the industry's very core.

But what happens when the moral compass spins out of control? The consequences are grave. A market where trust becomes as elusive as a mirage creates a desert of doubt, where clients tread with trepidation and deals disintegrate into dust. Word of unethical practices spreads like wildfire, scorching reputations and ruining careers. The long-term viability of any real estate professional hinges on their reputation for honesty and transparency.

[Every month every agent gets sent the state Real Estate Commission Bulletin, a regular catch up of what is happening in the industry. The first thing many of us do when we receive it? Head down to the 'Disciplinary Action' section where you can see every agent who has officially gotten themselves into trouble, might have lost their license etc.]

So, how does one navigate these perilous waters with honor intact? The solution, though simple in theory, demands discipline in practice: adherence to a stringent ethical code. This code must be a beacon that guides every action, from the grand gestures to the minute details. It is the unwavering commitment to do right by clients, colleagues, and oneself.

To translate this into action, we must first educate. Real estate professionals must immerse themselves in the ethical standards set forth by governing bodies and associations. Training programs, workshops, and ongoing education are the bedrocks upon which this knowledge is built. With understanding comes the power to apply these principles in every transaction.

Transparency is the next vital step. Like the clear waters of a serene lake, transparency allows all involved to see the depth of their decisions. Why get on the diving board to jump into the water below, if it's only one foot deep? It involves clear communication, the disclosure of all relevant information, and the steadfast avoidance of deception. This approach not only fosters trust but also cements the agent's reputation as a paragon of integrity.

But the proof, as they say, is in the pudding. Let us look to the past to predict future outcomes. Ethical agents have been shown to enjoy more referrals, repeat business, and a network that sings their praises. In contrast, those who stray from this path often find themselves mired in legal battles, their careers languishing in the shadows of their misdeeds and likely are not currently in the industry right now.

While the golden rule of treating others as one wishes to be treated is a good starting point, the real estate industry requires a more tailored approach. Alternative solutions include the enforcement of stronger penalties for ethical breaches and the public recognition of agents who exemplify ethical conduct, thereby setting a standard for others to follow.

Imagine a world where every real estate transaction is a tapestry woven with threads of integrity. This is a world where agents are not just sellers of properties but custodians of trust. It is a world where 'Selling Sunsets' is not just about, shoes, clothing, gin and tonic and the exchange of land but about nurturing the seeds of confidence that bloom into long-term relationships.

So, as you stand on the threshold of this reality, ask yourself: Will you be the standard-bearer of ethics in real estate, the guardian of a legacy that values honesty over expedience? Your answer to this question may very well shape the horizon of your career and the landscape of the industry for years to come. Remember, in the realm of real estate, ethical selling is not just a must—it's the foundation upon which enduring and elongated success is built.

Every State Is Different

In the grand theater of real estate, where the stage is as vast as the nation itself, every state presents its unique script, its own set of rules and characters.

From the sunny shores of California to the historic streets of New York to the center of America, Davidson, North Carolina, the nuances of selling homes are as varied as the landscapes themselves. Know that every state has different legal and licensing laws, which should be adhered to at all times.

This will be the shortest section in this book, because although it might be obvious, we wanted to take the time to specifically state (*pun included*) that although bricks and mortar are still those anywhere across America, how they transfer ownership dependent on location can be wildly different.

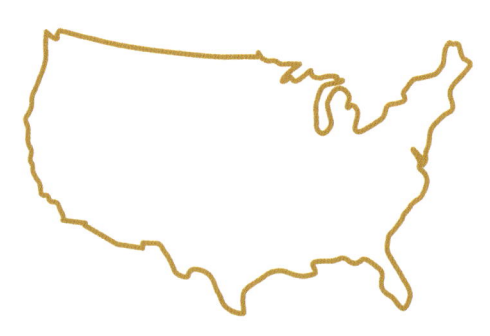

Chapter 4: The Journey to Licensure

The Licensing Exam: A Blueprint

The sun was just peeking over the horizon, casting a warm glow on the pages strewn across the desk. Each page held a promise, a step closer to a dream many aspire to but few achieve—becoming a licensed real estate agent. The journey to selling sunsets is paved with determination, knowledge, and the ability to navigate the complex waters of the licensing exam. This chapter is your compass, your map to the treasure, if you will. It's not just about answering questions; it's about understanding the terrain, mastering the elements, and emerging victorious, license in hand.

The objective here is clear: to conquer the real estate licensing exam. This is not just a test; it's the culmination of your hard work, a rite of passage into the world of gleaming properties and satisfied clients. But before you stand at the summit, you must embark on the climb. This part of the journey is non-negotiable.

Step one - choose the right real estate school for you. Upon writing this book, most of these schools will offer either in class learning, or entirely online or even a hybrid option. This is a hard choice as you will likely not know the teacher, their style, how the school will do their best to help you pass, we have recommendations for you, but ultimately it will be on you to pass the school and the test, so let's explore that process...

Now to really begin, you'll need a sturdy base camp—equipping yourself with the necessary prerequisites. You'll need a comprehensive understanding of national real estate principles and practices, along with the laws and regulations specific to the state where you intend to practice. Textbooks, practice exams, and real estate courses are your gear; make sure they are up to date and comprehensive.

Imagine the exam as a mountain with several paths to the top. Some are steep and direct, while others meander through complex legalities and tricky scenarios. Let's take a broad overview of these paths: they start with property ownership concepts, wend through contract law, financing principles, and market analysis, before scaling the heights of agency relationships and property disclosures.

Now, let's delve into the detailed steps. Begin with property basics—types of ownership, land use regulations, and valuation methods. Grasp them not just with your mind, but with your hands. Feel the texture of deeds in your fingers, the weight of zoning laws in your arms. Next, master the intricacies of real estate contracts. Understand every clause and condition as you would know the lines on your palm.

As you prepare, remember this: the exam is not just a test of memory, but of understanding. Can you apply the concepts to real-world scenarios? Can you navigate the labyrinth of financing options, from mortgages to government loans? What of ethics and professional practices? These are the sinews and muscles of your climb.

Amidst all this preparation, some practical advice: do not merely skim the surface of subjects. Dive deep. Engage with practice questions that challenge your grasp of the material. And a warning: beware the alluring but dangerous trap of procrastination. It is a crevasse that has claimed many.

Listen attentively in class, whilst the test [from my experience] is written to confuse and trick you, the teachers with the good schools genuinely will do what they can to ensure you pass both the school test and the state and national test.

But how will you know if you're ready? Testing or validation comes from practice exams. Score consistently above the passing threshold to ensure you're prepared for the real thing.

Should you encounter difficulties, like concepts that elude your grasp or persistently low practice scores, don't despair. This is where troubleshooting becomes vital. Seek out a study group, a tutor, or additional resources to fortify your understanding.

Are you beginning to visualize success? Can you see yourself, standing at the peak, the vast landscape of opportunity spread out before you?

Do you feel ready to commit to this journey? Can you allocate the time, the energy, the focus?

You must. Because those who dare to conquer the licensing exam hold the key to unlock doors to magnificent properties, to guide others to their dream homes, and to bask in the glow of sunsets they sell.

Remember, every question answered correctly is a step up the mountain. And every concept understood is a personal victory—a vista of knowledge conquered, a horizon expanded.

In closing, let's ponder a thought from the great mountaineer, George Mallory. "The first question which you will ask and which I must try to answer is this, 'What is the use of climbing Mount Everest?'" For us, the answer lies not in a mountain, but in a license. The use is to achieve a dream, to reach a goal, to sell not just houses, but homes.

From experience we would say very little learnt from the real estate pre-licensing course will truly set you up for success. There is little to no discussion about how to market yourself, how to get business, the true fundamentals of being a successful real estate agent, however...

The licensing exam is not just a test; it's the blueprint of your career in real estate. Study this blueprint, understand it, and the homes you sell will not just be structures. They will be the canvases of sunsets, the settings of lives well-lived. Your journey begins now. Are you ready to take the first step?

Choosing Your Brokerage

To navigate these treacherous waters, the solution is equally clear: ongoing education and professional development. By embracing continuous learning, you ensure that your sails are always catching the latest winds of change, propelling you forward.

Implementing this strategy begins with a commitment to education. Seek out courses that not only satisfy continuing education requirements but also enrich your understanding of the industry. Delve into seminars on the latest marketing techniques, enroll in workshops about cutting-edge technology, and attend conferences that bring thought leaders to the fore.

As you chart this course, remember—the sea of knowledge is vast. To prove the value of this pursuit, consider the success stories of agents who've embraced continuous education. They speak of expanded networks, increased sales, and a deeper sense of confidence in their craft. They are the agents with thriving careers, the ones who not only react to change but anticipate it.

Could there be other solutions? Certainly. Mentorship programs, peer-to-peer learning, and self-directed study are all worthy vessels on the journey to professional mastery. Yet, they are tributaries, not the river itself. The main current must be a structured, intentional approach to ongoing education.

Real estate brokerages come in various forms, each with its unique culture, resources, and market presence. A large franchise might loom like a skyscraper, its shadow falling far and wide, promising a certain prestige and an established business model. Contrastingly, a boutique firm might resemble a custom-built home, offering a personalized touch with a focus on local markets. The significance of this choice cannot be overstated—it's crucial to align with a brokerage that reflects your values, complements your working style, supports your growth and most importantly have the most successful peer mentor who wants to show you the ropes and nothing but success for you.

Why compare these disparate entities, you might ask? Because in understanding the nuances between them, you gain insights into the industry's inner workings and into your own aspirations. This knowledge serves as the foundation upon which you will build a successful career.

The criteria for comparison are manifold: market reach, support and training, company culture, commission structure, brand recognition, and niche specializations, to name a few. It is against these benchmarks we measure the worth of each option.

As we dive into the direct comparison, you'll notice the similarities that bridge the gap between the giants and the gems. Both large franchises and boutique firms can provide a sense of community, opportunities for mentorship (always stated, not always followed through), and avenues for professional development. They each, in their own way, offer a home for your ambitions.

Yet, when we pull the lens back, the direct contrast is stark. Large franchises boast extensive networks, robust training programs, and sometimes global brand presence. They often provide powerful marketing tools and a well-oiled machine to back your efforts. In contrast, boutique firms offer a more intimate environment, one where your voice is heard, your style is recognized, and your presence is not just another number. They might provide a closer-knit community and opportunities to make a direct impact on local markets.

This chapter does not include visual aids, but imagine if you will, a chart with two columns—one for franchises, the other for boutiques. Each row lists the criteria mentioned, and as you mentally check off which aspects resonate with you, a clearer picture forms of where your future lies.

The analysis of these options yields profound insights. A large franchise might be the wind beneath the wings of an agent who thrives on brand power and structure. Conversely, a boutique firm could be the fertile soil for those who wish to grow organically, to carve out a unique market niche.

Connecting these theoretical comparisons to the contemporary relevance, consider this: the real estate market is ever-evolving. In an age where personal branding and digital marketing are paramount, does the allure of a franchise's brand recognition outweigh the flexibility and adaptability of a boutique firm?

Picture yourself walking through the doors of your future brokerage. Can you see your name etched on the glass of a towering skyscraper, or painted on the window of a quaint, street-side office? Where do you feel your dreams taking root?

Let's not forget the cadence of this decision—it's not to be made in haste. Take the time to visit brokerages, to speak with agents who have chosen each path. Seek out the stories behind their successes and their struggles. What rhythms do you hear in their narratives? Which beat matches the pulse of your ambition?

In conclusion, ponder this: In choosing your brokerage, are you seeking the might of a franchise's thunder, or the whisper of a boutique firm's breeze? Whatever your choice, let it be one that resonates with your personal brand and aspirations, one that amplifies your voice in the chorus of real estate professionals.

The brokerage works for you. It's something commonly understood but never discussed or delved into. There are very few brokerages who will not accept any real estate agent fresh out of school and the difference between being a number and a genuine partner is a line of questioning we would always recommend having directly with the company owners.

Will the company explain their benefit under their branding and marketing? If so, ask yourself is every single agent within that brokerage successful? If the benefit of the branding was that lucrative, every agent would equally be as successful.

As the morning sun fully unveils itself, casting its golden light on your future, remember that your brokerage is more than a name—it's your partner in the dance of selling sunsets. Choose wisely, for this partnership will shape the horizons of your career and the lives of those you will one day serve.

Are you ready to make the choice? Will you be the one to harness the strengths of your chosen brokerage, to carve out a reputation as luminous as the sunsets you sell? The decision is yours, and the next chapter of your journey awaits.

Continuing Education and Growth

In the dynamic tapestry of real estate, each thread—each skill, contact, and piece of knowledge—interweaves to create the vibrant pattern of your career. But the industry is a creature of change, a chameleon constantly shifting under the sun's relentless journey across the sky. Have you considered the full implications of this evolution on your path to selling those coveted sunsets?

The real estate landscape is not static, and neither should be your education. The problem at hand is clear: agents who fail to adapt to new trends, technologies, and legalities risk becoming relics in a modern, fast-paced market.

Fortunately or unfortunately depending which side of the fence you sit, as mentioned before, each state will require mandatory continuing education classes every single year. So, "technically" every agent is receiving training every year, this is mandated, not optional, but some might say the knowledge attained within to help your business is too.

So what might befall the unprepared agent? Their knowledge grows outdated, their methods antiquated, and their services less relevant in the eyes of the discerning consumer. In an industry where trust is the cornerstone of every transaction, falling behind is not an option—it's a professional death sentence.

Yet, when we pull the lens back, the direct contrast is stark. Large franchises boast extensive networks, robust training programs, and sometimes global brand presence. They often provide powerful marketing tools and a well-oiled machine to back your efforts. In contrast, boutique firms offer a more intimate environment, one where your voice is heard, your style is recognized, and your presence is not just another number. They might provide a closer-knit community and opportunities to make a direct impact on local markets.

This chapter does not include visual aids, but imagine if you will, a chart with two columns—one for franchises, the other for boutiques. Each row lists the criteria mentioned, and as you mentally check off which aspects resonate with you, a clearer picture forms of where your future lies.

The analysis of these options yields profound insights. A large franchise might be the wind beneath the wings of an agent who thrives on brand power and structure. Conversely, a boutique firm could be the fertile soil for those who wish to grow organically, to carve out a unique market niche.

Connecting these theoretical comparisons to the contemporary relevance, consider this: the real estate market is ever-evolving. In an age where personal branding and digital marketing are paramount, does the allure of a franchise's brand recognition outweigh the flexibility and adaptability of a boutique firm?

Picture yourself walking through the doors of your future brokerage. Can you see your name etched on the glass of a towering skyscraper, or painted on the window of a quaint, street-side office? Where do you feel your dreams taking root?

To navigate these treacherous waters, the solution is equally clear: ongoing education and professional development. By embracing continuous learning, you ensure that your sails are always catching the latest winds of change, propelling you forward.

Implementing this strategy begins with a commitment to education. Seek out courses that not only satisfy continuing education requirements but also enrich your understanding of the industry. Delve into seminars on the latest marketing techniques, enroll in workshops about cutting-edge technology, and attend conferences that bring thought leaders to the fore.

As you chart this course, remember—the sea of knowledge is vast. To prove the value of this pursuit, consider the success stories of agents who've embraced continuous education. They speak of expanded networks, increased sales, and a deeper sense of confidence in their craft. They are the agents with thriving careers, the ones who not only react to change but anticipate it.

Could there be other solutions? Certainly. Mentorship programs, peer-to-peer learning, and self-directed study are all worthy vessels on the journey to professional mastery. Yet, they are tributaries, not the river itself. The main current must be a structured, intentional approach to ongoing education.

[From our earliest days in real estate, brand new out of school, I remember sitting in training at my brokerage which was being taught from a teacher who had sold less homes that year than I had. Retrospectively and to this day, we are firm believes at the top level that it is just as important who you are learning your craft from, than it is the **what**].

Now, envision the agent who has taken the helm of their learning. Their words resonate with authority; their strategies reflect the most current of methods. They are the ones who clients seek out, knowing they will receive the most informed and effective service. This agent is not a relic but a beacon, guiding others towards success.

Let's consider the rhythm of your career. Is it not similar to the ebb and flow of the market? The quiet lulls and sudden surges mirror the need for both reflection and action. In the quiet spaces, seek out knowledge and personal development. When the market surges, apply it with vigor.

Imagine the vivid scene: a room full of eager learners, the air charged with the electricity of potential. You are among them, absorbing every word, every concept. You are not just attending another obligatory course; you are investing in your future, sharpening your edge in a competitive field.

Does this not excite you? The thought of becoming an agent who not only sells properties but sells them with unmatched expertise and insight?

In a profession where your reputation is your most valuable asset, let education be the jewel in your crown. It is not enough to rest on the laurels of past achievements. To sell sunsets, you must glow with the knowledge of the present and the promise of the future.

Remember the industry statistics of how many agents leave the industry within the first two years.This book and Barry Pulver as the author is on a firm mission to change that, through experience and through example. The importance of mentorship is paramount, coupled with the right systems, tools and education, the only limitation in your business is looking back at you in the mirror.

Conclude this thought with a direct question to yourself: Will you be the agent who watched as the industry passed them by, or the one who rode the crest of innovation to new horizons?

Choose to be the latter. Commit to your continuing education and growth. Let each day be an opportunity to learn something new, to strengthen your foundation in this ever-evolving world of real estate. And as you do, watch as the sunsets you sell become the backdrop to a career that's as brilliant as the fiery skies you promise.

Chapter 5: Choosing the Right Fit

Understanding Your Goals and Values

In the kaleidoscopic world of real estate, where the promise of luxurious properties and the allure of lucrative deals reflect in every polished surface, it is easy to get lost in the shimmer. However, the savvy agent knows that a successful career is about more than just selling sunsets; it's about aligning one's personal compass with the magnetic north of their professional environment. In this chapter, we will explore the critical intersection of personal and professional goals and values, and how this alignment is the bedrock of a rewarding real estate career.

To navigate this landscape with integrity and purpose, one must first chart their course. The list that follows is a beacon, illuminating the components that merge personal aspirations with professional ethos.

1. Identifying Core Values

2. Setting Long-Term Goals

3. Understanding Brokerage Culture

4. Aligning with Ethical Practices

5. Building a Brand Around Values

6. Evaluating Personal Growth Opportunities

1. Identifying Core Values

The bedrock of any enduring structure is its foundation, and so it is with the architecture of a career in real estate. What are the values that anchor you? Integrity, accountability, diligence, or perhaps community involvement? Understanding these intrinsic motivators is critical, for they are the silent partners in every transaction you undertake.

Consider the testimony of a seasoned agent, Alex, who recounts a pivotal moment: "Early in my career, I realized that my drive for environmental sustainability was non-negotiable. This epiphany shaped my decisions, leading me to a brokerage that prioritized green living spaces and eco-friendly practices." Alex's story is not unique but a testament to the power of values in guiding career trajectories.

Practical applications of this knowledge are manifold. When values are clear, they inform your interactions with clients, shaping not just the deals you pursue but how you negotiate them. A value-driven approach sets you apart, establishing a reputation that magnetically attracts like-minded clients.

This is of the most importance and is likely to be completely unique to you and you alone. A lot should be expected from any brokerage or company where you 'hang' your license, but first you must look inwards so you can do the right due diligence on the outside.

2. Setting Long-Term Goals

Where do you see yourself in ten years? It's a deceptively simple question, yet it holds the keys to your future. Long-term goals are the stars by which you navigate the vast ocean of real estate opportunities. Without them, you're adrift, subject to the currents of the market.

To illustrate, meet Serena, who dreamed of creating a community-focused brokerage. "The vision was clear," she shares. "Every decision, every partnership was a stepping stone towards that goal." Serena's clarity in her long-term objectives was the compass that led her to success.

Bringing theory into practice, setting concrete milestones towards your goals enables you to track progress and make necessary course corrections. These goals also communicate to prospective brokerages where you're headed and why you might be an asset to their team.

If you take us up on our offer after going through this entire read, when we discuss you and your business 1-on-1 we will dive in detail into a few different accountability documents we created. These go from a strong focus on your next 12 months, but also remembering and stating what your long term goals are. There is a caveat, as (again) the amazingly high fall out rate for new agents, shows that action and mentorship need to be prominent in the early stages establishing your business... to have the ability to navigate to and strive for those long term ambitions.

3. Understanding Brokerage Culture

Anchors and stars aside, the vessel you choose to sail with is just as important. Brokerage culture is the wind in your sails—it can propel you forward or leave you floundering. A brokerage's values, mission statement, and work environment should resonate with your own principles.

"I wanted a culture of collaboration, not cutthroat competition," says Miguel, a top-performing agent. His experience underscores the importance of finding a brokerage whose culture amplifies your strengths and supports your approach to business.

Practical application of this insight involves research and engagement. Attend brokerage events, speak with current agents, and immerse yourself in the brokerage's community initiatives to understand their culture. The fit must be mutual for the partnership to thrive.

Highly advised as well is to go on your intuition and gut feel for what and what you hear. As mentioned earlier, if every brokerage had the best culture and was as amazing as (they all) say they are, then every single agent would be successful there. A powerful reminder that sometimes if you have a barometer (of this sounds like.. you know… to me) you might want to listen to it.

4. Aligning with Ethical Practices

Integrity is not just a personal virtue but a professional mandate. Aligning with a brokerage that upholds ethical practices is non-negotiable. After all, trust is the currency of real estate.

Evidence of a brokerage's ethical standards can often be found in their handling of difficult transactions. Reflecting on a challenging sale, veteran agent Priya recalls, "The brokerage stood by its commitment to transparency, even when it meant losing a deal. That integrity earned us a loyal client base."

In practice, working with a brokerage that mirrors your ethical stance means fewer conflicts of conscience and a stronger, more trustworthy brand.

It is highly unlikely whether you would know this right now and sometimes through experience (both good and bad) you will see this and sometimes learn this. Initially, especially in real estate, some company's are guilty by association, so have a look at the agents to admire, are friends of yours and certainly who added to and wrote this book and look at where their conduct their business with and why.

5. Building a Brand Around Values

Your brand is your promise to the world, a distillation of your values into a recognizable and reliable persona. In the ever-changing tapestry of real estate, a strong brand is a consistent thread.

"Your brand is your legacy," asserts Elias, a broker known for his community involvement. "It's what people remember when the open house signs are put away."

The practical application here is strategic branding. Every marketing material, every client interaction should reflect your core values, reinforcing your brand and attracting clientele that appreciates what you stand for.

In 2023 the 'power' of a real estate brokerage is very much second fiddle to the 'power' and personal brand of an individual real estate agent or team. Use this to your advantage! Look at brokerages who are empowering those individual brands and those who's very own logo is still front and center of every single listing sign.

For me, when I created The Exceptional Brand back at the end of 2017 when I was really looking to embrace my own personal brand, from that moment when I took action on it, my personal business sky-rocketed. The funniest part though was for every listing appointment and agreement I went through, the number 1 question asked by the home seller was "why am I selling with eXp Realty as it says here, I thought I was working with you?" [Real estate education moment - every listing / agreement is technically with the firm you are with not with you] That was the biggest eye opening in this industry for me and since that moment, we started to create a powerful mission to education the top agents (who typically were already aware) and even brand new agents (including you reading this book) the very importance of the agent and not the brokerage.

6. Evaluating Personal Growth Opportunities

Lastly, a brokerage should not just be a platform for sales but a crucible for personal development. Opportunities for growth are as crucial as the commissions.

Reflect on the words of Eva, an agent who found her calling in mentorship: "The brokerage's emphasis on professional development allowed me to discover my passion for coaching new agents."

In practical terms, seek out brokerages that offer training, mentorship programs, and avenues for advancement. A brokerage invested in your growth is a partnership that values your potential.

You need to know how you work best, if you do not know this just yet, then go back to the first point and remember who you are and what your personal values are. Growth opportunities are always out there and believe us when we say that not all companies are what they appear, but there are still successful agents at every company, that is always very important to remember.

As we cast our gaze across the tranquil waters of opportunity, let us not forget that the most beautiful sunsets are those witnessed nor just from Netflix, but from the shores of our own aspirations, reflecting the values we hold dear. Align your goals with a brokerage that understands this, and together, you will not just be selling sunsets, but crafting legacies... for you, your business and your family.

Researching Potential Brokerages

Embarking on a career in real estate is akin to navigating a labyrinthine market, with each turn presenting new challenges and opportunities. Selecting the right brokerage is paramount, as it becomes your vessel through the unpredictable seas of property transactions. In this crucial chapter, we delve into the art of researching potential brokerages, ensuring that you anchor yourself to an agency that not only sails in tandem with your professional ethos but empowers you to conquer new horizons.

The journey of a thousand miles begins with a single step, and the first stride in our expedition is understanding the essence of a brokerage that aligns with one's aspirations. The claim we lay out is clear: by meticulously researching and evaluating potential real estate brokerages, an agent can lay the cornerstone for a flourishing career that is both fulfilling and profitable.

The fundamental evidence supporting this claim stems from industry statistics and market analysis. A study conducted by the National Association of Realtors indicates that agents affiliated with brokerages that offer comprehensive training programs and robust support systems are 75% more likely to achieve sustained success in their first five years than those who do not. If this is 75% of the 20% left in the industry after two years then this becomes even more scary. Repeating a prior mention earlier in the book, just remember it can be just as important who you are learning from as it is what you are learning.

Yet, to truly appreciate this evidence, we must delve deeper into the nuances of what these training programs entail. These range from in-depth courses on market trends, to hands-on workshops on negotiation and sales tactics, to advanced tech platforms that streamline the buying and selling process. The brokerage's investment in its agents' education is a direct investment in its own success, creating a symbiotic relationship where both parties thrive.

Of course, there are counterarguments that suggest the individual agent's grit and determination are the sole determinants of success, regardless of the brokerage's support. While personal tenacity is undoubtedly a vital ingredient, it is the nurturing environment of a supportive brokerage that often catalyzes this drive into tangible achievements. A rising tide lifts all boats remember and believe us (from experience) it is quite honestly just more fun to do things and achieve success together and not be fighting against an internal brokerage headwind,

In response to such counter-evidence, we highlight the importance of company culture—a factor that can significantly amplify an agent's natural abilities. Brokerages that foster collaboration, celebrate successes, and encourage innovation provide fertile ground for agents to bloom. These elements, when coupled with personal ambition, create a powerhouse for success.

Adding to the repository of supporting evidence are testimonials from agents who have experienced transformative growth within such nurturing environments. These narratives are not mere anecdotes but lifelines of wisdom, illuminating the path for those who follow.

Finally, as we reach the conclusion of this exploration, we assert with reinforced conviction that the right brokerage is not just a place of employment but a harbor for professional development. It is where ambition is met with opportunity, where training is paired with technology, and where culture synergizes with character.

However, among the constellation of brokerages that dot the real estate firmament, one name commands particular distinction: eXp Realty. As the #1 global team leader within the ranks, I felt it would be a potential disservice to the start of your career if I didn't spend a minute explaining a few home truths. Why does eXp stand as the pinnacle of brokerage excellence? The answer lies in its revolutionary approach to the industry, track record and transparency in an industry where sometimes brokerages look as hazy as the skies we see watching Selling Sunset.

eXp Realty transcends traditional brokerage models with its innovative cloud-based structure, offering agents unparalleled flexibility and autonomy. The company culture is steeped in collaborative success, evidenced by its virtual office environment that connects agents worldwide for networking and mentorship. Training is a cornerstone of eXp's ethos, learning from the very top agents who provide all the training, sharing what what they are currently using to be top agents in their market. The new local mentor program, in addition to having on-going and direct business partnership from the very best in the business is something we honestly wish we had when we first got our real estate license.

But beyond the training and the culture lies a suite of technological tools that revolutionize the buying and selling experience, from cloud-based transaction management to cutting-edge data analysis software. This commitment to innovation positions eXp agents at the forefront of the industry, equipped with the knowledge and tools to excel in an ever-evolving landscape. Without ever mentioning the internal iBuyer programs, incredible healthcare offerings and (at current) 9 free lead generation tools. [For much more and a factual based discussion you can schedule a call directly at www.ScheduleThatChat.com]

In this chapter, we have journeyed through the meticulous process of researching potential brokerages. We have presented evidence, countered skepticism, and ultimately, revealed why eXp Realty emerges as the bastion of real estate excellence. But remember, any agent can be successful at any company and there is always a reason that there will be a few brokerages still around and available. As an agent aspiring to sell sunsets and forge a legacy, the choice becomes clear: align with a brokerage that not only promises growth but delivers a horizon brimming with potential.

Interviewing Brokerages

As you step into the world of real estate, choosing the right brokerage can be as crucial as finding the right property for your client. The brokerage you align with can significantly impact your career trajectory. It's more than just a place to hang your license; it's a decision that will shape your professional development, income potential, and market presence. It's time to master the art of interviewing brokerages, equipping yourself with the right questions and insights to make an informed decision that aligns with your ambitions.

Before embarking on this quest, it's imperative to understand what you're looking for. Taking us back to earlier in this chapter, if you need to revisit if before we continue, do it without hesitation. Do you desire robust support, a collaborative environment, or perhaps a place that offers cutting-edge technology? With this clarity, you can approach each interview with precision, ready to uncover the layers that constitute the brokerage's core offerings.

Let's preview the key areas you need to probe during your interviews:

- ↣ **Commission Structures**
- ↣ **Training and Support Services**
- ↣ **Technological Advancements**
- ↣ **Market Presence and Branding**
- ↣ **Culture and Community**
- ↣ **Growth and Scaling Opportunities**
- ↣ **Recognition and Rewards Programs**

Commission Structures

The commission split is the bread and butter of your income. It's essential to grasp the specifics of how a brokerage structures its commission arrangement. Is it a fixed percentage, a sliding scale, or capped after a certain threshold? Ask for examples to illustrate how the split would work in real-world transactions. This transparency will give you a clear picture of your potential earnings.

Agents often share their experiences with different commission models. Some prefer the simplicity of a fixed split, while others thrive under a system that rewards high performance with a more favorable split. Research testimonials and connect with current agents to get a sense of the prevailing sentiment towards the brokerage's commission structure.

Imagine closing a deal on a luxurious beachfront property. Under brokerage A, you might take home a standard 70% of the commission. With brokerage B, however, after surpassing a sales threshold, you keep 90%. Which model suits your goals and work ethic? Understand these scenarios to make an educated choice.

Numbers are one important factor but less so than value. Our friends over on Selling Sunset start with splits of 50% and do you know how many agents are banging on the owners door to be hired? Whatever you were thinking, at least double it! So whilst splits are important, ask yourself and that company exactly where the value is for the company's part of the commission and if they say the company's reputation... run and run fast! (unless you are trying to get on the Netflix show, that is quite valid). In this day and age, capping (*where you have the ability at a certainly threshold to make close to 100% of your commission*) should be your baseline, honestly too, so should be ownership in the very company you are working for, through share holding / other ownership.

Training and Support Services

In the rapidly evolving real estate market, ongoing training is non-negotiable. It's the scaffolding that supports your climb to the top. Inquire about the frequency, depth, and breadth of the training programs offered. Are there mentorship opportunities? How does the brokerage keep its agents at the forefront of industry changes?

Agents who have benefited from exceptional training programs often credit their success to these initiatives. Seek out stories of agents who have experienced significant growth due to the support and learning opportunities provided by the brokerage.
Consider how a well-structured training program could enhance your skills. For instance, a comprehensive negotiation workshop could empower you to secure better deals, directly affecting your success rate and client satisfaction.

Do not be afraid to hold back from asking about accountability, actual tangibles about what this all would look like for you and the success level of those who will be providing the training for you. Every brokerage will talk a great game, but ask to see blue prints, speak with former agents of that company, ask why they left and when it comes to mentorship as we have mentioned before, this is the most important part of your early steps in real estate so ask great detail.

Technological Advancements

A brokerage's technological offerings can streamline your workflow and enhance your marketing strategies. Ask about the CRM systems, data analytics tools, and virtual tour capabilities they provide. How does the brokerage stay ahead of the tech curve?

Brokerages that invest in technology often have a track record of increased agent efficiency and client engagement. Look for data or case studies that showcase the benefits of their tech platforms.

Imagine having access to a state-of-the-art CRM that automates your follow-ups and keeps you organized. This could free up time for you to focus on closing deals and expanding your clientele.

Personally, I remember at the very beginning of 'Covid' March 2020, when life seemingly shut down, business did and the world did not know what had happened and more importantly what was going to happen. For us, we had (and now have a more evolved) a virtual office which was accessible from anywhere in the world. The amount of phone calls from friends I had in the industry who needed help, didn't know what to do was astounding... as for us, our training, support and company continued like normal. One step further, I had the honor of expanding eXp Realty to the UK (*the first ever international expansion*) a few months earlier and the UK was shut down for business for much longer than the United States. Had it not have been for those initial months, my team and eXp UK might not have had the **record breaking** success due to seamlessly being able to continue, with the internal operations.

Technology might not be the most important factor in choosing your real estate brokerage, but from our experience in can be **pivotal** even when you might not be expecting it.

Market Presence and Branding

A brokerage's market presence used to bolster your own. Find out in modern times, how the brokerage positions itself in the market. What are their marketing strategies, and how would they benefit you as an agent? Remember internal collaboration and support are fantastic, but if a house next to the office is going to be listed next week, realistically you and all the agents in the office will be competing against each other for the business.

Strong branding can distinguish an agent in a crowded marketplace. Agents affiliated with well-respected brokerages used to enjoy a halo effect, but with the importance and direct access from agent to customer / potential client, this has changed. Investigate how the brokerage's reputation has enhanced its agents' success.

What is going to be the biggest part of your branding on business cards, listing signs, open house signs etc. is it your name and logo? Is it your brokerages? When you step into the coffee shop for your first client meeting, is that client expecting you or the company owner? When Sally down the street from you calls your phone to come and list her house, did she call your brokerage phone number or the one in your pocket?

Culture and Community

Culture is the heartbeat of a brokerage. It's about the values, attitudes, and practices that permeate the organization. How does the brokerage foster a sense of community? What are their core values?

Agents thrive in environments where they feel supported and aligned with the company ethos. Seek stories that highlight the brokerage's community spirit and collaborative culture.

Envision yourself as part of a team where camaraderie and mutual support are the norms. This conducive environment can significantly impact your job satisfaction and motivation.

Can you create your own culture and community within the brokerage? Some of the initiatives we had had a hand in creating internally, we are often told have transformed people's businesses and even lives. Listen, I get it, day one (where we only know what we know) we have the intimidation factor and inferiority complex, but let's not forget those long term goals we were just speaking about. Look at the brokerage and see what new innovations have happened recently as a result of direct agent input.

I will never forget back at the end of 2019 launching eXp Realty in the UK as eXp UK was running a roadshow around the country announcing the launch and traveling, hundreds of miles in the same cars, the same hotels as the brokerage's leadership. I know not many will ever have the opportunity to do so (will you?), but you will never learn as much about the truth ethos of peoples and a company as when you are in such close and consistent company, one of the biggest learning experiences of my professional life.

Growth and Scaling Opportunities

Your career goals should align with the brokerage's vision for growth. How does the brokerage support agents looking to expand their business? Are there systems in place to facilitate scaling, such as team-building or leadership opportunities?

Find examples of agents who have successfully grown their operations within the brokerage. How has the brokerage contributed to their expansion?

Little personal sidebar here (*again, I know, sorry but not reall that sorry*) when I joined my brokerage I did so for two reasons, do have mentorship I never had received before and to finally build my own personal brand. Fast forward little over a year and I never would have imagined that I would have expanded the company outside of North America and become a team leader of a network which has expanded into six continents. The reason I joined the brokerage? No. But the very sheer opportunity or partnering with a like-minded company with big growth and scale ambitions? Yes. Always look to be fully in alignment.

Picture yourself leveraging the brokerage's resources to build your team and amplify your reach. The right brokerage should make this vision attainable. Even more exciting in this day and age where you (*yes **you**, reading these very words*) and I have the ability to do this **together**.

Recognition and Rewards Programs

Rewards and recognition can be powerful motivators. What programs does the brokerage have to acknowledge outstanding achievements? Are there incentives that align with your personal goals?

Agents who feel **appreciated** often have higher levels of engagement and loyalty. Gather testimonials that reflect the positive impact of the brokerage's recognition programs.

Imagine the **pride** of being recognized at the annual awards gala, solidifying your status as a top performer. This recognition can enhance your reputation and drive you to reach new heights.

Now, imagine 20 years later at the latter part of your career, you open the drawer by your desk and you have 45 certificates on pieces of paper and 3 trophies, how does that make you feel? Proud would be one understandable answer, but compare that to a brokerage where (*in addition to the award recognition*) your success and accomplishments has been rewards by shares in the company, how does that make you feel? Furthermore, how does that make your family and future generations feel?

Transitioning to the next chapter of your real estate career is an exhilarating journey. As you interview potential brokerages, keep these points in mind to ensure you find a home that not only meets your current needs but also fosters your **future growth**. Remember, the right brokerage is a partner in your success, providing the foundation upon which you can build a **thriving** and fulfilling career.

Considering Mentorship and Support

In the bustling world of real estate, the lure of selling sunsets is often entwined with the harsh reality of cutthroat competition and complex transactions. For neophytes, navigating this landscape can be akin to a sailor trying to chart a course through uncharted waters. Without **guidance**, the journey risks ending in a shipwreck rather than a treasure discovery.

The challenge facing new real estate agents is substantial: mastering the intricacies of property law, understanding market fluctuations, and cultivating a network of clients all demand a level of expertise that takes time to develop. But what if there was a compass to guide you through the stormy seas?

The consequences of neglecting to seek mentorship and **support** are manifold. Without a seasoned captain to steer the ship, new agents may find themselves adrift, making unnecessary **mistakes** that can be costly, both financially and professionally. The attrition rate in the industry is telling; many promising careers sink before they ever truly set sail.

The solution? Embarking on a voyage with a **trusted** mentor and tapping into robust support systems offered by real estate brokerages. A good mentor acts as a **beacon**, illuminating the path to success with their knowledge and experience. Brokerages with structured support programs provide the wind in your sails, helping propel your career forward.

To implement this strategy, seek out brokerages that are renowned for their commitment to mentorship. These are the organizations where seasoned professionals take fledgling agents under their wing, imparting wisdom and providing practical, hands-on guidance. This can take the form of regular **one-on-one** meetings, shadowing opportunities, or collaborative deals where you learn by doing.

But how does one measure the efficacy of such programs? The proof is in the pudding, or in this case, in the success stories of those who have walked this path before you. Testimonials of agents who attribute their rapid ascension to the insights and backing of their mentors are not hard to find. Brokerages that celebrate these stories often boast higher retention rates and an enviable number of **top** performers.

While mentorship is a cornerstone of success, it's not the only structure you can lean on. **Peer** support groups, **team** collaborations, and continuing **education** programs are alternative solutions that offer their own unique benefits. A brokerage that fosters a **culture** of teamwork and collective growth ensures that no agent is an island but part of a larger, synergistic archipelago.

What does this landscape look like when painted with the brush of vivid imagery? Picture yourself walking through a listing, your mentor at your side. They point out features of the home that you hadn't considered, share anecdotes of similar sales, and provide you with a proven strategy for pricing. This hands-on learning is invaluable; it's the difference between reading about sailing in a book and actually feeling the deck beneath your feet as you navigate the open sea.

Why, you might ask, should a seasoned agent invest time in your growth? The answer lies in the symbiotic nature of mentorship. Not only do you gain insights, but your mentor also benefits from fresh perspectives and the satisfaction of shaping the industry's future. It's a win-win situation, with the added bonus of strengthening the brokerage's reputation as a nurturing ground for excellence.

Take it from us, starting at the largest real estate brokerage (*at the time*) then moving to a uber niche boutique, ultimately landing at the final destination, there are many moving parts to consider. Retrospectively, we can say none of those are more important of the very foundation of mentorship, the who, the what and the why.

In conclusion, the journey from neophyte to seasoned real estate professional is fraught with challenges. However, with the right mentorship and support structure, the path becomes clearer. These programs are the lifeboats that keep your ambitions afloat, ensuring that when you finally reach the shore, you're not just surviving, but thriving. As you turn the page to the next chapter of your real estate career, remember that the most beautiful sunsets are those that are **shared**, not sailed alone.

Culture and Values

The very essence of a brokerage is encapsulated in its culture and values. It's the heartbeat of the organization, influencing every interaction and decision. When evaluating a potential brokerage, ask yourself: Do their values **resonate** with mine? Can I thrive in the **environment** they've cultivated? A harmonious **alignment** with a brokerage's culture can be the wind beneath your wings, propelling you towards a fulfilling career.

Detail Expansion

A brokerage's culture is its signature—distinct and telling. It's palpable in the way colleagues interact, in the leadership style of the management, and in the day-to-day operations. Seek out **testimonials** from current and former agents to get a sense of the real **atmosphere**. Are they collaborative or competitive? Is there a sense of **community** or does each agent operate as an island?

Evidence and Testimonials

You might come across a brokerage boasting a team-oriented culture, and yet, a closer look at agent testimonials may reveal a different story. Conversely, a brokerage that seems individually driven might surprise you with a strong support network behind the scenes. Look for **patterns** in these accounts—they are the signposts pointing you towards an authentic understanding of a brokerage's culture.

Emotional intelligence should always be at the forefront, understanding that there will always be biased and experiences in these testimonials which should not sway you. It can be difficult to remove **opinion** from **fact**.

Making the Final Decision

Embarking on a career in real estate is like setting out to conquer an ever-shifting landscape. As you stand at the precipice of choice, the brokerage you align yourself with can either serve as a launchpad for success or a **misstep** that you'll wish to retract and ultimately will. This chapter is dedicated to helping you navigate the process of making that all-important final decision.

Introduction to the List

Before you lies a decision of significant consequence: choosing the brokerage that will be your **home base**, your support system, and your gateway to success in the industry. The following list is your compass, guiding you through the critical considerations that will illuminate your path to the right choice.

Presentation of the List

1. Culture and Values
2. Training and Development
3. Commission Structure
4. Market Presence and Branding
5. Support and Resources
6. Technology and Innovation
7. Growth Opportunities
8. Clientele and Market Specialization

Point Elaboration, with our words of wisdom from our experiences...

Culture and Values (*continued*)

Practical Applications

Imagine walking into an office where your achievements are celebrated, where there's always someone to turn to for **advice**, and where leadership is **approachable**. Contrast this with a place where you're just another number, isolated and disconnected. Which environment would you prefer to nurture your career? The answer lies in the **cultural** fit. [Remember the personal story about traveling around a foreign country with the leadership of the brokerage? Not the norm, but an experience that speaks *volumes*]

Seamless Transitions

As important as the cultural milieu is, the **practical** aspects of your career trajectory cannot be overlooked. Let's shift our gaze to the **tangible** tools and knowledge that will shape your professional development....

Training and Development

The real estate market is dynamic, and continuous learning is your lifeline. A brokerage that invests in your growth through **training** and **development** programs is not just enhancing your skill set; it's laying the foundation for your longevity in the industry.

Do you want to learn from the best in your market? What about the best in the country and world? While markets may be different, **people** at their core and sales principles remain similar enough for you to take training from the best in any market and utilize it to help your business.

Detail Expansion

Look for a brokerage that offers a robust curriculum, ranging from licensing courses to advanced marketing strategies. **Evaluate** the **quality** and **relevance** of their training materials—are they updated regularly to reflect market trends? Are there **opportunities** for mentorship and one-on-one coaching?

Who are you learning from? Who is taking you under their wing? What tools and systems are there to directly bring you business?

Evidence and Testimonials

Agents who have excelled in their careers often credit their early training as a **pivotal** factor. Speak to top performers and inquire about the role their brokerage's training played in their success. These stories are the proof of the pudding, illuminating the path that lies ahead for you.

Training and Development (*continued*)

Practical Applications

Envision yourself a year from now, armed with a wealth of knowledge and strategies, confidently navigating complex transactions. This is the power of **comprehensive** training and development—it turns potential into expertise.

Seamless Transitions

Your first day in the real estate office, Selling Sunset is playing on the TV and everything looks pretty easy right? You turn up, open the door, show the home, camera follows you around, offer send in at $10 million, offer accepted, pay day next week... result!

When we say you need a mentor (*see the very last part of this book upcoming*) you need a mentor. We all need training from the best of the best, direct mentorship 1-on-1 and the ability to be in a frame work and brokerage which support personal and professional growth. When you have this, you will know. Your success will also be following very closely behind.

Commission Structure

The topic of commissions is often met with trepidation, but it's a critical element of your decision-making process. Understanding the commission structure is key to ensuring your financial goals align with the brokerage's policies.

Detail Expansion

Commission splits vary widely across brokerages. Some offer higher splits in exchange for monthly fees, while others may provide lower splits but cover marketing and administrative costs. Delve into the details—what is the long-term financial impact of these structures on your income? Do not be afraid to question where the 'value add' is in the commission the company is taking.

Evidence and Testimonials

Agents are typically forthcoming about their satisfaction or discontent with commission structures. These firsthand accounts are invaluable, exposing the realities beneath the surface promises.

Commission Structure (*continued*)

Practical Applications

Remember in 2023's (*Season 7, yes really, there are 7 seasons*) season of Selling Sunset, the newest agent to the office had a buyer (*in the region of*) looking for a house for tens of millions of Dollars and questioned her commission split structure? Let's say that commission split is close to 50% of the overall commission, it's her own buyer that she new prior to real estate, so does she deserve more? It's also her very first real estate transaction of her career, will she require a lot of direct and help navigating the waters? There is always two sides to every story...

Seamless Transitions

While money matters are crucial, so is the way you and your listings are presented to the world. Let's transition to the topic of market presence and branding.

Brokerage Branding vs Personal Branding

Practical Applications

A brokerage's brand used to the paramount to agents getting business, now it is the power of personal branding and the agent who is the defining factor. Does the company put a strong emphasis on their the brokerage winning you business or do they **empower** you, the agent to grow your brand and own business? The answer to these questions *should* speak volumes.

Detail Expansion

Evaluate the brokerage's marketing efforts and the strength of its branding. Do they have a recognizable logo, a personally branded professional website for you? How about solid social media game plan for you to grow your brand? These are the tools and help that will help you stand out in a crowded market.

Evidence and Testimonials

One of the biggest thoughts successful agents say retrospectively when they look back at their career is "I wish I would have focused on my own branding earlier". It's always easy to say from a level of success and experience looking back, but there is a lot of truth in these thoughts, one to consider from pre-day one.

Brokerage Branding vs Personal Branding (*continued*)

Practical Applications

Imagine handing a business card to a prospective client. Is it the same template as every one else or is it something that screams you and your brand? The hardest part of real estate is standing out from a overly saturated industry, so do your part to be **unique**, be you.

Seamless Transitions

A strong personal brand is a beacon that draws clients, but the day-to-day support from your brokerage you receive is what keeps your ship steady in turbulent waters.

Support and Resources

The level of support and resources a brokerage provides can be the difference between floundering and flourishing.

Detail Expansion

Assess the availability and quality of administrative support, marketing resources, and legal assistance. Does the brokerage have systems in place to help you manage your workload and facilitate transactions smoothly?

Evidence and Testimonials

As a reminder if every brokerage was as great as they will flat out tell you, every agent there will be successful. A mirror and self-reflection should be a constant in your real estate journey but in the back end, the support, mentorship, training and systems to put it all together should be your glue that holds your back-end together.

Support and Resources (*continued*)

Practical Applications

You have a six hour working day, with two listing appointments, one buyer consultation, one closing and one negotiation to handle. Fortunately you have a one hour slot you have carved out for self-improvement and education, where is this hour best used? The choice is yours, at one office you have one class where you can catch 15 minutes within your allotted schedule, taught by someone who only has had two listings all year. Or you can choose from five live courses each by agents who currently have thirty plus active listings. Added to that, the recorded training from prior live training is available at your request. See those busy roads leading to your first office? That doesn't impact your one hour slot for option two.

Seamless Transitions

In an industry that's rapidly evolving, staying ahead of the curve is not just an advantage—it's a **necessity**. This brings us to the role of technology and innovation in your decision.

Technology and Innovation

In today's digital age, a brokerage's technological prowess can significantly enhance your efficiency and reach. We discussed earlier the difference between working and not working at the start of 2020, a time of life never imagined or planned for, but retrospectively pivotal.

Detail Expansion

Investigate the technology tools and platforms the brokerage offers. Are they leveraging cutting-edge CRM systems, virtual tour software, and data analytics to stay ahead? These innovations can streamline your processes and give you a competitive edge.

Evidence and Testimonials

Agents who have harnessed the power of technology often report higher productivity and client satisfaction. Their experiences highlight the transformative effects of these tools on their business.

Technology and Innovation (*continued*)

Practical Applications

Picture yourself using state-of-the-art tools to manage client relationships, market properties, and analyze data. The right technology can turn these tasks from burdens into blessings.

Seamless Transitions

While technology propels you forward, the opportunities for career advancement ensure that your trajectory remains upward.

Growth Opportunities

A brokerage that provides avenues for professional growth is a garden in which your career can bloom beyond comprehension.

Detail Expansion

Scrutinize the opportunities for advancement within the brokerage. Are there clear paths to leadership roles or niche specializations? A brokerage that encourages and facilitates your growth is investing in your future as much as you are. What about earning income in other areas or avenues? Not something taught through real estate schools but very available currently and more so going forward.

Evidence and Testimonials

Listen to the stories of those who have climbed the ranks within their brokerages. Their journeys are testaments to the fertile ground provided by their firms for career advancement. Are there common themes behind their stories and journeys? Typically success leaves clues.

Growth Opportunities (*continued*)

Practical Applications

Envision yourself assuming greater responsibilities, perhaps even leading a team or becoming a specialist in luxury properties. These are the milestones that a brokerage with ample growth opportunities can help you achieve.

Remember the personal story of why we joined the brokerage we partnered our business with? It was for the peer mentorship available in addition to the creation of our own personal branding. At that point, as a single (*and fairly new*) agent, there was no plans or blue prints to expand into a team leader locally, let alone in over fifteen countries and six continents. Living by the very definition of growth opportunities, you too will get to a level where the blueprint we (*maybe even **you***) created is one that you own, are proud of and directly look to link arms and share with others.

Seamless Transitions

As you consider your upward mobility, reflect on your goals, who you are, the specific clientele and markets you wish to **serve**.

Clientele and Market Specialization

Aligning with a brokerage and individuals that specializes in your desired market segment can be a catalyst for success.

Detail Expansion

Determine whether the brokerage and mentor has a strong foothold in the type of real estate that interests you. Whether it's residential, commercial, luxury, or a specific neighborhood, a brokerage with specialized expertise can provide you with invaluable insights and connections.

Evidence and Testimonials

Agents who have aligned their passions with their mentor's and brokerage's specialization often express greater job satisfaction and success. Their alignment allows them to become experts in their chosen niche, attracting the right clientele and closing more deals. One company might have three hundred or even thirty agents per location, the importance of that true mentor who has the time and desire to help you one-on-one reigns supreme. Especially when they have trod down the path and road you envision and desire to go down.

Clientele and Market Specialization (*continued*)

Practical Applications

Imagine becoming the go-to agent for waterfront properties or downtown lofts because your mentor has empowered you with specialized knowledge and marketing tools. This is the advantage of a focused market specialization.

In Closing...

In the end, the decision you make will shape your future in the real estate industry. It's a choice that requires **careful** consideration, reflection, and a bit of soul-searching. As you weigh your options and envision your path forward, remember that I, Barry Pulver, am here to serve as a resource and guide. My experience and insights are at your disposal, meant to light your way as you embark on this exciting and rewarding journey. Together, we will ensure that the sunsets you sell are not just transactions, but milestones in a **thriving** career built on a foundation of informed decisions. Taking us to the end here and our final parting gift to you...

Chapter 6: Making the Sale - The Art and Science

Time Out

You are half way through the latest episode of Selling Sunset, you have seen one house and on the fifth argument over (insert fabricated drama here) you need to take a pause and we feel in this book we are at the same place. No drama, but a lot which goes into your new career before you have decided that this is your new career and you have even officially got your real estate license in hand and active.

This 'time out' chapter will get into more of the specifics of working inside the industry and what you have to look forward to after you have gone through the appropriate steps and outline that the majority of this book entails.

Enjoy some of what you have to look forward to...

Mastering the Showing

As this book is written at the end of 2023, the very beginning of the 'downfall' (*we would say shift*) of buyer agency is likely to change how real estate is operated in America forever. In the author's opinion at the time of writing, counter-lawsuits are inevitable but regardless of the immediate outcome, let's look ahead to 2030 (*at the latest*) and buyer agency **will** be conducted in as similar way to how our partners in Australia operate. Possible even going further into a more European model like our partners operate in the UK. Either way, this section of the book more than any other will be drastically changing and with very strong business all over the world, we are already situated and best positioned to help you get ahead of the curve and changes even as a brand new real estate agent.

That said, let's unpack on the current real estate pre-licensing school and activity and methods of buyer agency...

Unlocking the door to a property, you can almost feel the anticipation in the air – the unspoken promise of potential that whispers through the halls. Whether you're a seasoned real estate agent or a newcomer to the game, the art of the showing is a pivotal skill in your arsenal, one that can transform a casual viewer into a committed buyer. A showing is more than a mere walk-through; it's a **performance**, a dance between the possibilities of a space and the desires of a client.

Your objective is clear: to weave a narrative that not only highlights the strengths of the property but also **aligns** seamlessly with the aspirations of the prospective buyer. But how do you achieve this artful alignment? What tools must you have at your disposal, and what steps must you follow to ensure each showing is a masterpiece?

First, gather your materials. You'll need a deep knowledge of the area and property's features way before you show the house. A keen understanding of your client's needs, and a touch of showmanship to bring it all together. Ensure you have access to all areas of the property, that lighting is optimal, and that any accompanying materials, such as property details or floor plans, are on hand and immaculately presented.

The process begins with preparation. Study the property's layout, its unique features, and its potential drawbacks. Consider the buyer's profile – what are they looking for in a home? What might turn them off? The answers to these questions will guide your narrative.

Now, let's dive into the detailed steps. Start by setting the stage. Before the client arrives, ensure the property is pristine and inviting. Open the curtains to let natural light flood the space, and, if appropriate, light a scented candle or start a fire in the fireplace to create a cozy atmosphere. This first impression is crucial; it sets the tone for the entire showing.

As the client steps through the door, greet them with a warm smile and a firm handshake (*or alternative appropriate greeting*). Establish a connection. "Can you imagine yourself sipping coffee on that balcony every morning?" This kind of open-ended question engages the client's imagination right from the start.

Lead them through the property, highlighting key features. Don't just tell them about the new kitchen appliances; show them how smoothly the drawers close, how the surfaces gleam under the lighting. In the living room, don't just mention the view; pull back the curtains and let them take it in, let the space do the talking, silence can be a secret weapon, use it.

Throughout the showing, offer practical advice. Remind them of maintenance tips for the garden, or suggest how they might furnish an awkwardly-shaped room. Caution them about overlooking areas that need future investment, like an old roof or outdated wiring.

Validation comes with the client's reactions. Watch their body language, listen to their comments, and encourage them to envision living in the space. If they start discussing where they'd place their furniture or how they'd entertain guests, you're on the right track.

Should issues arise – perhaps the client is concerned about the size of the bedrooms or the lack of a garage – be ready and armed with **solutions**. Suggest how a particular room could be extended or how nearby amenities compensate for any perceived shortcomings.

Your sentences flow like the melody of a well-rehearsed song, some punchy and sharp, others smooth and lingering, creating a rhythm that is both engaging and informative. "The garden blooms in spring," you say, pausing to let the mental image blossom, "a tapestry of color."

Incorporate dialogue to add **authenticity**. "The previous owner adored this kitchen," you might share. "They'd spend hours here, crafting meals for family gatherings."

Show, don't tell. Instead of simply stating the house is spacious, lead them into the open-plan living area and let them feel the expansiveness. Describe the echoes of laughter you can almost hear bouncing off the walls during a festive dinner party.

Conclude the showing by inviting questions and providing clear, concise answers. Leave them with a vivid picture, a sense of home that lingers in their mind long after they've left. "Imagine the memories you'll create here," you say as you hand them a brochure, the pages a promise of dreams yet to be fulfilled.

And there, with the door closed and the echo of footsteps fading, you'll know you've mastered the showing, turning a mere visit into a vision of the future, and, with hope, a buyer into a homeowner. Always leaving with a next stop or follow up discussed, agreed upon and scheduled.

Negotiation Tactics for Winners

In the realm of real estate, the ability to negotiate effectively is not just a skill but an art form—the brushstroke that turns a prospect into a buyer, a listing into a sold sign. As we delve into the intricate dance of negotiation, remember that the key to a successful outcome lies in the subtle balance between assertiveness and empathy, strategy and intuition. Let us embark on a journey through the tactical landscape that ensures you and your clients emerge victorious in the vast marketplace of real estate.

Before we explore the strategies that define master negotiators, it is crucial to understand the significance of this skill set. Negotiation is the heartbeat of every real estate transaction, the moment where desires are translated into **deals**. It is a delicate balancing act where understanding the **psychology** of the buyer, the seller, and the market itself can mean the difference between a mediocre agreement and a triumphant one.

1. **Preparation is Power**
2. **The Mirroring Technique**
3. **The Anchoring Effect**
4. **The Art of Concession**
5. **The Final Offer Play**
6. **Psychological Leverage**

These strategies, when understood and applied with **finesse**, can elevate your negotiation prowess to new heights.

No warrior enters the battlefield without understanding the terrain, and no negotiator should enter discussions without thorough preparation. This means doing your homework on the property, the location, the market conditions, and, most importantly, the people involved in the transaction. Gather as much information as possible—knowledge is your currency.

Having comprehensive knowledge about the property includes understanding its history, potential, flaws, and unique selling points. Market conditions encompass not only current trends but also predictions for the future. Regarding the individuals involved, learn their motivations, their must-haves, and their deal-breakers. This information will guide your approach and inform your strategy.

A study by the Harvard Business Review highlights that negotiators who spend more time preparing can increase their chances of a successful outcome by as much as 11%. Testimonials from seasoned agents also underscore the importance of preparation, with many recounting instances where a deal was salvaged by a previously uncovered piece of information.

[In more recent times, I have gone into listing appointments armed with nothing but a pen and paper. Madness? Perhaps, but the genuine confidence in local knowledge, the property and especially our marketing in any home allowed more presence and less distractions with the standard listing presentations. Now, for the record, each of these listings we won and we sold, and honestly I believe there is something to be said for being 100% **present**, genuine and listening to your potential client and their needs!]

Imagine advising a client to hold off on accepting an initial offer because you're aware of upcoming infrastructure projects that could boost property values. Or, conversely, recommending a seller to close quickly due to an impending market downturn. Preparation gives you the foresight to make such impactful recommendations.

Moving gracefully into our next strategy, let's examine the mirroring technique. This involves subtly mimicking the behavior, speech patterns, or body language of your counterpart. It's a powerful way to build rapport and encourage openness.

The act of mirroring can create a subconscious bond, making the other party feel understood and connected to you. It's not about imitation, which can come off as mockery, but about establishing a harmonious communication rhythm. For some specifics on this used at the highest level, look up Chris Voss.

Research in the field of psychology has shown that people who are mirrored are more likely to view the person mirroring them as likable and trustworthy. Real estate agents who have employed this technique often share stories of how mirroring helped them break down barriers and foster a more collaborative negotiation environment.

When a client leans back in their chair, you might do the same. If they use certain phrases or terminology, sprinkling those words into your dialogue can enhance the sense of camaraderie. It's these subtle cues that can ease tensions and pave the way for a more agreeable negotiation.

The anchoring effect is a cognitive bias that refers to the human tendency to rely too heavily on the first piece of information offered when making decisions. In negotiations, this translates to the power of the initial offer.

Your first number sets the stage for all subsequent negotiations—it becomes the anchor from which all other figures will be compared. This doesn't mean you should start with an outrageous price or demand, but rather a thoughtfully considered one that aligns with your client's goals while leaving room for negotiation, if needed or realistic.

A study by Northwestern University found that the final price of a negotiation is typically closer to the initial anchor than the counteroffer. Real estate agents have shared numerous anecdotes where an effectively placed anchor has led to a final sale price beyond expectations.

Imagine you're representing a seller in a strong market. By setting a higher anchor, you can give yourself a cushion that allows for negotiation while still achieving a sale price that delights your client. Conversely, as a buyer's agent in a buyer's market, a lower anchor could secure a purchase well under the listed price.

Our logic and part key to our success has been to stray away from the real estate game in principle and price appropriately from the outside. One of the best pieces of advice and statistics taught early on in our journey, whilst working at a luxury auction company was that there are only three reasons a property does not sell;

1) **Price**
2) **Condition**
3) **Marketing**

Some of these factors you can control more than others, but bringing it back full circle to earlier comments, always strive to find the win-win for all, set the right expectation (yes, even in list price) and you will see the results you are looking for.

Now, let us turn to concessions. The art of concession involves giving something up in negotiations to gain something else. It is not a sign of weakness but a strategic move that can strengthen your position.

Concessions should be planned and executed purposefully. Every give should be with the intention of a get. It's important to understand the value of what you're conceding and what you expect in return. Concessions can also be used to test the waters and see how the other party reacts, providing valuable insight into their priorities.

Experienced negotiators often speak of the reciprocity principle, where a concession from one side is typically met with a concession from the other. This principle is well-documented in negotiation literature and serves as a fundamental rule in achieving compromise.

For instance, you might concede to a lower commission rate in exchange for a longer exclusive listing period. Or, you might agree to leave certain high-end appliances in a home in exchange for a quicker closing date. Each concession is a carefully considered chess move that brings you closer to checkmate.

Approaching the endgame, the final offer play is a tactic used to signal the conclusion of negotiations. It involves presenting what is framed as the absolute last and best offer, almost always used when there are multiple interested parties in buying the house.

The final offer play is a **psychological** tool that implies a take-it-or-leave-it scenario. It should be used sparingly and only when you genuinely believe that negotiations have reached their limit. This tactic can push the other party to seriously consider the offer, fearing the loss of the deal altogether.

Agents who have successfully used the final offer play recount the heightened tension it creates and the relief when it results in an agreement. This tactic is often the climax of the negotiation narrative, bringing a sense of urgency and finality to the table.

Imagine you're in a multiple-offer situation, and your buyer is on the brink of losing out on their dream home. A well-timed final offer, that you initiate. positioned as the best they can do, may just tip the scales in your favor, compelling the seller to act rather than risk losing a strong buyer.

Finally, let's explore psychological leverage. This involves using **emotional intelligence** to influence the negotiation outcome in your favor.

Understanding the emotional drivers behind the other party's decisions can provide powerful leverage. Is the seller sentimentally attached to the home? Is the buyer under time pressure? Such insights can guide your approach, ensuring you address their emotional needs as well as their financial ones.

Negotiations often hinge on more than just numbers; they involve people's lives and dreams. Agents who leverage emotions effectively often share stories of how they've turned challenging negotiations around by tapping into the human element.

Consider a situation where the seller is nostalgic about their home. Highlighting how your buyer appreciates the home's character and will cherish it as the seller has can make a compelling emotional appeal, potentially swinging the negotiation in your favor.

In the world of real estate, the power of negotiation cannot be overstated. It is the invisible hand that guides the market, the silent dialogue between desire and fulfillment. Through the strategic use of preparation, mirroring, anchoring, concessions, final offers, and psychological leverage, you can craft a narrative of success for both you and your clients.

Remember, negotiation is the art of finding **common ground** in a field of diverse interests. It is the harmonious blend of tactics and empathy, of strategy and sincerity. As you close the pages of this chapter, let the concepts and stories herein not just inform you, but inspire you. The next time you sit across the table, ready to negotiate, know that with these tactics, you hold the keys to unlocking the door to winning outcomes. Can you feel the anticipation, the promise of potential, as you prepare to sell not just sunsets, but dreams?

Closing the Deal

As the sun dips below the horizon, casting a golden glow over your latest listing, you stand at the precipice of a defining moment in real estate—the closing. The art of negotiation has brought you to the edge of success, but now, you must navigate the final, crucial steps with the same precision and skill. The closing is not merely an endpoint but a culmination of strategy, preparation, and finesse. Here, every detail matters, and every action is a stroke on the canvas of your career, a testament to your ability to not just sell sunsets but to finalize the dreams they represent.

You have journeyed through the complexities of negotiation. Now, let's chart the course through the closing process, where the abstract becomes concrete, and promises transform into signatures. The goal is clear: to ensure a smooth transition of ownership that leaves all parties satisfied (even happy if possible!) and your reputation as a closer unassailable.

To begin, you must gather the necessary materials and prerequisites: a ratified sales contract, a list of agreed-upon repairs (if any), home inspection reports, title insurance, mortgage approval and paperwork, and a closing agent. Each is a vital cog in the machinery of transaction completion.

A broad overview unveils the path ahead. The stages include finalizing the mortgage, conducting a title search, obtaining insurance, completing a final walk-through, and, at last, signing the closing documents. Then ultimately heading back to your office, gonging the huge bell and sharing the video to Instagram, right? But let's delve deeper, for in the details lies your success.

Finalizing the mortgage is a dance of numbers and deadlines. Your clients must provide their lender with all required documents and meet specific financial requirements before the loan is approved. Be the guiding force, the beacon that ensures they navigate this process without faltering. Let's be honest, this is not an enjoyable experience, whatsoever, but it is also a necessary part of the equation, unless you are working with cash transactions. Be the resource of frustration when needed (*and yes sometimes it is needed*) but more importantly, ensure you remind your client why they are going through these painstaking and tedious steps of the process. Don't be afraid to send them photos, ideas, videos and information that will remind them why the excitement is there and attempt to remind them to keep that front and center.

Conducting a title search and obtaining insurance may seem like mere formalities, yet they are shielded ramparts against future disputes. Confirm that the property's title is free of encumbrances and that a **reputable** insurance company is ready to issue a policy. These steps are your clients' armor in their new kingdom.

The final walk-through is a sacred ritual, a **last chance** to ensure that all is as it should be. Encourage your clients to scrutinize every corner, test every fixture. Should issues arise, be their champion, negotiating diligently for appropriate remedies.

The penultimate act is the signing of the closing documents. Here, your clients will sign their names more times than they can count, but with each signature, they inch closer to their dream. Be the steady hand that guides them through this marathon of paperwork, always ready to clarify and comfort.

Strategically placed tips and warnings are your gifts to the client. Remind them that closing costs must be accounted for, and they may vary. Caution them against making any major financial changes between mortgage approval and closing—such actions can and often will derail the entire process. Be the resource of education for them in this, any good mortgagor or lender will do this too.

The testing or validation of a successful closing is simple yet profound: keys in hand, smiles all around, and the satisfaction of a job well done. It's the moment when "sold" becomes more than a sign; it becomes a reality. *Selfie time?*

In the rare event that problems arise, your **troubleshooting** acumen must come to the fore. If financing falls through, have backup lenders at your disposal. Should the title reveal issues, work with a skilled attorney to resolve them swiftly. Every problem has a solution, and your role is to find it. One of the keys to success in real estate is adaptability, especially in the 'worst case' scenario category. As with the importance of intense research and due diligence before going to a listing appointment or showing homes, the more work you do in the front end will almost always work in the long run.

Have you considered the gravity of your task? The closing is the crescendo, the final note in the symphony of selling. It requires diligence, patience, and an unerring eye for detail.

Remember, the deal isn't done until the documents are signed, the funds are transferred, and the keys change hands. This is the moment of truth, where your hard work pays off, and your clients' dreams take physical form. Can you feel the anticipation building, the excitement of a closing well-executed?

In the grand tapestry of real estate, each closing is a thread that weaves your legacy. As you guide your clients through this final chapter, take pride in your role as a facilitator of futures, a crafter of conclusions. For in every closing lies the potential for a new beginning, a new story to be told beneath the vast, unfolding canopy of selling sunsets.

Chapter 7: Our Gift to You

We are Here for You

Firstly thank you for reading this book, more than anything else we hope it has provided some insight, wisdom and clarity on whether you really do want to enter the game of real estate. Yes, we do say game, as we can tell you (and as you will be fully aware of by now) it is a particularly lucrative career and opportunity, but with the amount of no's and rejection you are likely to get along the way, seeing it as a game... frankly makes it more fun.

One final offering, which yes costs on the open market much more than the price of admission of this read... we wanted to offer you a 1-on-1 30 minute call directly with you.

The summer of 2022 I was challenged by a former leadership coach of evaluating the cost per hour of my time and services and this experience was a very intriguing and eye opening one... BUT with the very purpose of creating this book was to be a resource, guide and speak from our experience in the real estate industry and offer insight, mainly objectively, that ultimately will help you decide whether real estate 'is' or 'is not' for you.

So if you choose to take us up on the offer, you can reach out directly to Barry Pulver (*not hard to find*) or go yourself onto www.ScheduleThatChat.com and quote this book and offer and we will have additional resources and tools at the ready.

As a final farewell as we will cast an eye on series 17 of Selling Sunset looking for you to walk in the office, we will bid our adieu with the wise Yoda from Star Wars...

"Do. Or No Not Do. There Is No Try"

Printed in Great Britain
by Amazon